THE POWER OF
STUDENT
AGENCY

THE POWER OF STUDENT AGENCY

Looking Beyond Grit to Close the Opportunity Gap

Anindya Kundu

Foreword by Pedro A. Noguera

Teachers College Press

TEACHERS COLLEGE | COLUMBIA UNIVERSITY

NEW YORK AND LONDON

Published by Teachers College Press,® 1234 Amsterdam Avenue, New York, NY 10027

Copyright © 2020 by Teachers College, Columbia University

Book Cover Designed by Ligature Creative

Library of Congress Cataloging-in-Publication Data is available at loc.gov

ISBN 978-0-8077-6388-9 (paper)
ISBN 978-0-8077-6389-6 (hardcover)
ISBN 978-0-8077-7856-2 (ebook)

Printed on acid-free paper
Manufactured in the United States of America

For the parents, teachers, and especially students who relentlessly fight for the education they deserve, unwilling to let their dreams be deferred . . .

Contents

Foreword

In 2014, Anindya Kundu and I wrote an essay entitled "Why Students Need More Than 'Grit.'" The short article, which received a considerable amount of attention, served as our attempt to respond to and critique the growing interest in the concept of "grit." In 2013, psychologist Angela Duckworth had delivered a viral TED Talk and received a MacArthur Genius Grant for introducing this topic to the world. Her book, *Grit: The Power of Passion and Perseverance* (2016), became a bestseller, and the idea of grit become the new educational sensation. Advocates claimed that by promoting grit as an attribute, students could achieve at higher levels.

Several organizations, particularly "No Excuses" charter school networks like KIPP, soon announced that they were going to focus on the development of grit among their students. The idea proved to be particularly attractive to urban charter schools, many of which embraced the idea that by making grit central to their efforts to educate and *socialize* inner-city youth, academic and behavioral outcomes would improve.

The celebration of grit was in keeping with the ideas that had been embraced by KIPP and other No Excuses charter schools for many years. In his book *Sweating the Small Stuff: Inner-City Schools and the New Paternalism*, David Whitman (2008), a fan and advocate of No Excuses charter schools, articulated the core ideas behind the enthusiastic embrace of grit. He and others argued that the key to educating poor Black and Latinx kids was imparting (or if necessary, imposing) middle-class values through a new form of paternalism—the act of limiting a person's or a group's autonomy by someone in a place of power. According to Whitman, such schools have to teach kids "not just how to think but how to act, according to what are commonly termed traditional, middle class values" (p. 3). They would do this by inculcating "diligence, thrift, politeness and a strong work ethic" (p. 4).

The first time I heard Whitman articulate these ideas was when he and I served on a panel at an event sponsored by several major foundations that were funding education reform initiatives. Though Whitman was not an educator, he maintained that the No Excuses charter schools offered the best approach to improving outcomes and closing the achievement gap between middle-class White kids and low-income minority kids. He argued that the new paternalism, and grit in particular, was essential for educational progress.

I immediately took exception. My disagreement was based on the fact that as a kid, I too had grown up in the inner city, but my parents had worked hard all their lives, and so had many (though not all) other parents of the kids I went to school with. I also attended an Ivy League university (Brown) and had been educated with affluent White kids. I therefore knew from experience that many of them were not polite, thrifty, or hardworking. I resented the underlying assumption that poor kids or poor people were lazy and simply lacked a sufficient amount of "grit." Most of the people I had known while growing up worked hard. Many worked two or three jobs, sacrificed to support their families, and saved their money, but despite their efforts, most were still poor. They didn't lack grit. What they lacked was opportunity.

In the article Anindya and I wrote together in 2014, we pointed out that there were structural obstacles that limited the educational opportunities available to low-income students of color, such as overcrowded classrooms; underresourced, racially segregated schools; and lack of access to highly skilled teachers, to name a few. Similarly, outside of school, the neighborhoods where poor kids of color lived presented additional obstacles, including poverty, crime, violence, and toxic environmental conditions. All the grit in the world would not make a difference without a concerted effort to remove these obstacles, or at least provide kids with help in navigating around them. While we were not opposed to the idea that grit—persistence, a strong work ethic, stick-to-it-iveness, and so forth—is important, and that such qualities are indeed essential for kids to acquire, we rejected the notion that grit alone could overcome the obstacles. We argued against the idea that if more kids simply acquired grit it would be sufficient to improve the possibility for them to use education to achieve success.

Our article suggested that instead of grit, what low-income kids in the inner city needed was agency. This is the point that Anindya Kundu elaborates on further in his important, groundbreaking new book. To Kundu, agency is much more than grit because it is premised upon the ability to think critically about the obstacles a child may face. Rather than ignore the obstacles, Kundu shows that kids need help in figuring out how to navigate them. For example, if students feel compelled to go to work rather than to stay in school because they need to support their family, they might need counseling rather than stubborn persistence to help them figure out how to do both.

Anindya Kundu shows that, unlike grit, agency is based on the recognition that sometimes young adults, like his participants "Joe" and "Vanessa," need help. Rather than going it alone and relying strictly on individual effort and hard work, individuals with agency think critically about where and when they need help. Kundu shows how all individuals can develop social capital by acquiring mentors and utilizing social networks that provide access to critical resources, such as information about how to attain certain jobs and even health care services. Rather than doing it on their own, those who develop agency readily seek out advice and assistance from others with knowledge, connections, and experience about college, careers, and life in general. Young people with agency recognize that they may need financial, social, and emotional support to achieve their goals, and they are not too proud to ask for it. Most importantly, Kundu shows that rather than being an individual attribute, agency can be a collective one that makes it possible for schools, peer groups, nonprofits, or neighborhood organizations to contend with the structural obstacles that might otherwise thwart the aspirations and efforts of others.

Should not promoting agency be a larger focus in education?

Kundu draws upon the fieldwork he carried out with emerging adults of color from low-income, inner-city neighborhoods to demonstrate how they deploy agency to navigate obstacles that might otherwise limit them and trap them in a cycle of poverty. His attention to detail and his ability to establish trust and rapport with these young people makes it possible for him to obtain insights into the nature of their agency and how it developed over time, and to showcase agency's power to serve as a resource for overcoming obstacles. Not only does Kundu make agency a tangible concept, but in regular dialogue with Duckworth herself, Kundu has expanded the grit narrative to include more context, uncovering many social and cultural supports that allow a person to better tap into their grit.

Several of the chapters in this book elaborate upon the strategies these young people use to contend with the barriers they face. For this reason, Kundu's book is much more than simply an academic contribution to the vast literature on education and social mobility. If his core ideas are taken seriously, this book can serve as a resource to educators, policymakers, community advocates, and others who seek to address the educational needs of vulnerable and disadvantaged students. There are many young people throughout America who face challenges that are similar to those Kundu describes in this book. To prevent them from being undermined or consumed by these challenges, these young people will need much more than grit. If we want to see more of them succeed, they will have to develop a strong sense of agency.

—Pedro A. Noguera, University of Southern California

REFERENCES

Kundu, A., & Noguera, P. (2014). Why America's infatuation with "grit" can't solve our educational dilemmas. *Virginia Policy Review*, *11*(Summer), 49–53.

Whitman, D. (2008). *Sweating the small stuff: Inner-city schools and the new paternalism.* Washington, DC: Thomas B. Fordham Foundation & Institute.

Acknowledgments

This book has been a labor of love . . . mostly. At some points in time, it has felt like a bit of a slog, punctuated with moments of uncertainty and doubt. Taking dissertation research and turning it into a worthy "debut" book was not exactly a self-assured process for me, but, alas, here it is. This book may never have fully come to fruition without constant support and love from my family, close friends, and mentors. Just as it takes a village to raise a child, it took a village to raise this book to the shelves. And now that the seal is broken, I feel more confident that there might be another book in my future.

First, to anyone who has supported my work at all, a deep and heartfelt thank you for your patience and for believing in me. And thanks in advance for telling me that this book is quite illuminating and important! (I'm not sure how well sarcasm comes through in written prose.)

I must thank my mentors who continue to shape my career path and those who closely influenced the pages that follow.

Pedro, thank you so much for offering to write the foreword. What an honor. An endorsement from you cannot be taken lightly. You taught me that there are no shortcuts to gaining expertise and any subsequent respect, and that the journey to spread knowledge is a fulfilling one. Your scholarship has motivated me to be aware that there are high stakes to this work, which helps me remain passionate about connecting research to practice to help others.

Lisa Stulberg, thank you for your constant presence, from my decision to undertake doctoral studies through to my early career. You've been the glue that holds our program together at NYU. Thank you for taking the time, often without much warning, to chat with me and go over big decisions. I've learned from you that being good and doing good work should not be mutually exclusive.

Angela Duckworth, thank you for your enthusiasm and charisma, which are infectious, as is your desire to help kids live fuller lives. I'll always remember our first phone call when you said you had time to chat from the train, even though you were quickly becoming a household name. Collaborating with you has been the opportunity of a lifetime, not just because of the seriousness with which you conduct your work but also because of the kindness you bestow on others.

Next, I'll try to express what gratitude I'm able to put into words to my parents, Mita and Aniruddha Kundu. Thank you for your selflessness and for the sacrifices you made so that I could pursue my American Dream. Ma, thank you for your strength and for showing me how to be a caring and good person—and for always having told me that those are the most important accomplishments in life. Baba, thank you for having an incredible moral compass, which has been hard to follow at times given how steady it is. I hope to pass on everything I learned from you both.

To my sister and "third parent," Jayeeta: Again, thanks for always proofreading my work! But seriously, thank you for proofreading my life. Getting to see your example has been the most advantageous resource in my life. Tell Cedar that I have a similar appreciation for his brotherly advice. You are world-class mentors.

Other mentors and peers whom I would be remiss not to call out include Noel Anderson, for showing me how to have an impactful career in more ways than one; Jonathan Zimmerman, for showing me how to express research so that it engages with broad audiences; David Elcott, for warmly supporting my work without exception and without expectation; Cyndi Stivers and Katrina Conanan-Riel, for believing in me and amplifying my voice; Jaclyn Kelly and Heather Sutton, for showing me how to use research to assist mission-based organizations and the communities they serve; and Megan Staropoli, for being the kind of teacher I talk about in this book—one who changes your life for the better. An important thank you to some of my close friends, peers, and even some former students (who once felt I deserved a teaching award). You deserve a lot of credit as well for helping this project in various ways: Neil Dalal, Sarah Murphy, Mahari Simmonds, Colton Elliot, Colin Hennessy Elliott, Sam Ayala, Nasrin Jafari, Analisa Crosthwait, Angelina Quezada, Brittany Barnett, Sabrina Gill, Monet Jeffries, and Romie Williams.

And, of course, a hearty thanks to those who helped bring this book to life! Thank you to Julie Mosow for being an absolute dream editor to work with. I'm excited for our future collaborations and that someday-second book. Thank you to Matt Meier and the immensely talented graphic design team at Ligature Creative for creating a cover that is simple and compelling, and on budget for a budding academic. Thank you to the Teachers College Press team for seeing the value of this project and supporting it from start to finish. You have helped me create something that I'm proud of.

I've saved the most important person to close: my charming, brilliant, hilarious, and beautiful wife, Pamela Villa. Thank you for adding color to my life. I aspire daily to be someone worthy of your love.

Peace,
Anindya

Prologue

Welcome to American Dilemmas

In the fall of 2016, I walked into my classroom at New York University (NYU) ready to teach undergraduates for my third consecutive year. I was starting to feel more seasoned, finally over the initial teaching jitters of prior years, but some nights I still stayed up restlessly thinking about the interplay between current events and my ideas for the following day's discussion. Embodying a college lecturer required being a public speaker, a learning facilitator, and, occasionally, a guidance counselor to young people who were navigating a lot in their lives. On the other hand, I was also a busy doctoral candidate working toward my dissertation defense, so I welcomed teaching as a distraction and relief from that grueling process.

My course was titled American Dilemmas: Race, Inequality, and the Unfulfilled Promise of Public Education. Each morning, I woke up excited to carry the torch of my mentor, Dr. Pedro Noguera. Currently a dean of the University of Southern California (USC) Rossier School of Education, and one of the most influential education sociologists in the country, he had created this important course for NYU. In 2012, after a long day of work at the New York City Department of Education, I had decided to attend a seminar talk that Pedro was giving at NYU. Listening to him articulate issues around education and opportunity made me first consider changing the direction of my career from policy to research. The idea that I was trusted to teach Pedro's course, after being inspired by him to follow this path, was particularly meaningful to me.

The first weeks of American Dilemmas are a bit heavy and, I'll admit, can provide a generally pessimistic overview of the current state of public education in the United States. The course challenges undergrads to confront the rigidity of structural inequality and the reproductive nature of disadvantage. They must grapple with the idea that race, class, and other characteristics of students' backgrounds continue to be primary sorting mechanisms for success. Ironically, our American public schools are the places that are meant to be the primary institutions that the public expects will uphold our strong egalitarian values, promote opportunity, and curb our rampant social inequalities, but, sadly, the institutionalization of inequality is especially true for public school contexts, even though every student is supposed to get a "fair shake."

With NYU consistently ranking as one of the country's most expensive colleges, it is not a surprise that many of my undergraduate students come from privilege. Yet most seem to be humble and energized to affect the politics of the future. Together, we consider how race has been socially (as opposed to biologically) constructed throughout history. We talk about how skin color can still be used as a means for separation. We briefly look at the arbitrary nature of racial segregation, using the Jim Crow era as a historically relevant example: Jim Crow laws varied from state to state, with certain states considering a person to be Black if they were one-eighth Black and others setting the bar at one-sixteenth Black. Under these laws, being Black was not really about skin color at all.

I encourage the students to question why the achievement gap continues to remain so wide and so racialized today. How real is "meritocracy," the fluffy idea that the best and brightest will always prevail, if we can still somehow predict how a person's life will end up based on the zip code they are born into? Maybe what we're really talking about is an *opportunity* gap (Carter & Welner, 2013).

That was Noam Chomsky's logic when he critiqued the highly controversial book *The Bell Curve* (Herrnstein & Murray, 2010) by saying that attributing differences in people's academic success or IQ to differences in race was the same as attributing differing levels of academic success to differences in height.[1] Neither characteristic correlates with a real difference in a person's intellectual ability, which is a malleable and ever-evolving product of one's environment.

While today most people are reluctant to make arguments directly correlating race with intelligence, achievement, or motivation for fear of appearing bigoted, as I tell my students, the same people often have no problem making *cultural* arguments. The following are examples of the sentiments I hear, in places like coffee shops and bars, when I tell people about my research on minority students and how they overcome obstacles:

"A lot of the time, certain people don't *care* to take advantage of the multiple opportunities given to them."

"Those kids come from a culture of violence."

"Do you see those kids always loitering outside that school a few blocks away on Park Avenue? At lunch, they just hang out instead of being more involved in school."

Let's ignore for a second that "those kids," most of whom happen to be of color, likely do not have an adequate physical space (like a field or a park) to "hang out" in on their middle-of-Manhattan school campus. Instead, let's focus on the fact that the man who said this to me and who had associated these students' outward behavior with negative decisionmaking and value systems is a symptom of a larger, American problem. In later chapters, I will get to why these types of arguments are just plain shortsighted and sometimes simply thinly veiled racism, often reflecting a lack of understanding of what culture is. But mostly, in the moment, they frustrate me to no end because the person saying them may not actually be willing to have the extended discussion needed to unpack their logic. And even when they are willing, for those of us who sometimes have these types of conversations with others, we know how mentally exhausting they can be.

I tell my students that if they are open to it, they can share relevant, personal anecdotes of their own encounters with interpersonal or structural racism in their lives with their classmates.

One day, an incredibly shy and until-then silent Latinx student chimed in: "Before the first day of school, I asked my mom if I looked White enough to succeed at NYU. If my hair and my clothes fit in. I look around and mostly see White faces and I stand out." The class fell quiet as her statement soaked in. She was highlighting how race and the perceptions that surround it play into her day-to-day life—how race affects her sense of self and her ideas of what it takes to succeed in an elite, liberal learning environment.

Since that day I sometimes pause to wonder about the extent to which students really might need to look "White enough" to succeed at a place like NYU. Will professors be more receptive to their questions and critiques if they seem "White enough?" Will other students respect their opinions if they don't? The simple prestige and pressure of attending an elite university within an urban center might also lead to the pressures to conform to an abstract idea of "Whiteness." The same student later told me that she could feel herself prepare to embody a "Whiter" persona as she walked the short distance between the Lower East Side where she grew up to Greenwich Village, where campus is.

And so there are, in fact, environmental factors, which are largely out of their control, that may make minority students feel like they do not belong.

Once during my office hours in my first year as a lecturer, one of my Black students, Mahari, admitted to me that outside of class he had never had a conversation with a White classmate. This was during his first semester at NYU, and he told me later that it likely wasn't until his second semester that he had such an interaction. This was shocking to hear, but the more I thought about it the more I realized my initial shock was a function of willful ignorance. Mahari is extremely outgoing and was one of the standout individuals whom I have had the honor of having in class. I mentioned a bit of Mahari's story in my first TED Talk, titled "The Boost Students Need to Overcome Obstacles." What I didn't say in that talk was that he, too, overcame immense obstacles, like getting kicked out of his home and experiencing periods of housing instability, before eventually making it to community college and then NYU to finish his bachelor's degree in his mid-20s.

After doing a simple Internet search, I was surprised to learn that the student body of NYU was only about 5% Black, though the national Black population is about 14%. In New York City, it is around 25%. Of course, these students are bound to feel isolated at times when their college environment—one that will determine many of their future opportunities—does not resemble places they feel more included.

When I'm not teaching, I am an education sociologist researching how students who come to school with various social and economic disadvantages can harness their potential and nurture their "agency." Fundamentally, I define "agency" as a person's capacity to leverage resources to navigate obstacles and create positive change in their life. I will provide a more comprehensive and theoretical definition of agency in Chapter 2. *Fostering* someone's agency means helping them to help themselves.

My own students, many of whom are aspiring to be classroom teachers, administrators, or other education professionals, motivate me to do practice-driven research that challenges notions that some students are just deficient. Helping them to realize their own agency means getting to impact the future of education. Agency is the main subject matter of this book. Race and class are basically irremovable from this conversation, as they continue to be sources of marginalization in this country.

*

In later chapters, we will discuss the stories of my participants like "Tyrique," who did not grasp that he could leave a lasting legacy until he was inside a prison cell for armed robbery. After feeling aimless during his first year in jail, an older detainee took Tyrique aside to ask for help with a youth program. He needed a 22-year-old like Tyrique to influence and make a positive impact on incoming teens. Tyrique reluctantly accepted the responsibility, but in the process of engaging with people younger than himself, he discovered that he loved mentoring and started to realize his own potential.

All pictures of Tyrique and Vanessa by Sashko Danylenko

Becoming a mentor in prison changed Tyrique's trajectory. He joined other programs and took courses for college credit. In his Religious Studies class, he received his first-ever "A" on a paper. He asked his teacher if it was a mistake. It wasn't. He had written a great essay.

After Tyrique had served his time, he got a job with Fortune Society, a prominent nonprofit where many of the staff and executives were formerly incarcerated. In our interview, he said, "Now I had this idea: Like holy shit. You can go home and be an *executive* of something?" Today, Tyrique has a master's degree in social work and lectures at Columbia University, all while working full time, fighting mass incarceration, and being a great husband and father to three children.

In this book, I will share many other narratives from people who also beat the odds so that we can start thinking about what strategies can be implemented in educational settings for students who might face similar circumstances. You may find yourself relating to certain aspects of these stories. You might also start to draw your own connections between participants' narratives, perhaps seeing similarities between Tyrique's story, and that of someone like "Vanessa." As a child and adolescent, Vanessa moved between the homes of her extended family members, living in each of New York City's five boroughs, while her mother battled heroin dependence. During this unstable period, Vanessa became a teenage mother and dropped out of high school. However, her love of learning always remained. Within a couple of years, she felt motivated to get her GED and eventually attend community college.

Unfortunately, on top of everything else, Vanessa had been born with only one poorly functioning kidney. It failed right after she completed her GED and had enrolled in community college. She was forced to spend 10 years on dialysis during this educational transition. While she was on extended bed rest, she received continued support from her community college mentors, who had helped her apply to school and finish her associate's degree.

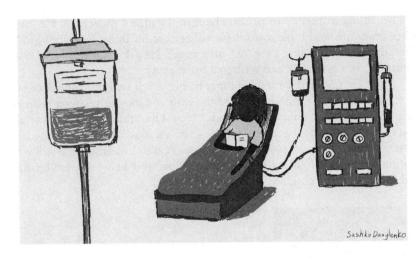

Sashko Danylenko

After a successful kidney transplant, Vanessa eventually completed a bachelor's degree from one of the most prestigious all-women's colleges in the United States. Today, Vanessa serves as a lead counselor for transfer high school students in New York who also hope to go to college, and she serves as a great example for her young adult son.

Even at their lowest points or amid their toughest challenges, both Tyrique and Vanessa were full of latent potential that just needed the right nourishment to bloom. Encouragement grounded in a thorough understanding of their unique personhood helped them to see themselves in a new and improved light and feel confident enough to pursue their newly developing goals. If our educational systems can offer students these types of simple yet powerful supports, rooted in fundamental respect for humanity, there is a lot to be hopeful for.

Sashko Danylenko

*

Through my work, I have learned that "disadvantages" do not have to be disabling. Once someone perceives and acknowledges certain limitations or hurdles, those challenges can then be reframed as opportunities to reflect and develop new goals. Understanding obstacles this way can actually enhance someone's ability to become more successful because it deepens competencies and motivation, something that may not be experienced by people who have had more and easier access to opportunity.

If schools and educators are able to capitalize on this premise, celebrating both individuality and diversity, perceived differences can be used to empower students. (There are schools that primarily serve low-income students of color that do this well, and I will discuss them in Chapter 6). If looking "White enough" is actually something that is tied to achieving academic success, our schools and education systems are failing our diverse student bodies. However, if more schools addressed issues of race (or class, or gender, or sexuality, or any other traits used to marginalize) rather than avoided them, students might not feel that their unique identity makes them inferior but rather more than capable of achieving success in life.

Generally, common sense might dictate that one obviously doesn't need to "look White" to succeed. But why does this feel obvious, especially when decades of research (related to education, health, and employment) shows Whiteness to beget better rewards? Perhaps the guise of obviousness is deeply rooted in our own ideologies—our mainstream values, specifically those of individualism and meritocracy that run so deep through our U.S. blood that we believe these ideas reflexively.

In his book *In Defense of Elitism*, cultural critic William Henry wrote, "The measure of a just society is not whether a demographically proportional share of any group succeeds, but whether any individual of talent can succeed regardless of what group he [or she] belongs to" (Henry, 1995, p. 15). Though the idea of any individual having the potential to succeed sounds like an idea everyone can support, the truth is that we are surrounded by an unreasonable amount of disproportionality, which, to some extent, is enforced by state instruments. Statistics show that one in three Black boys is bound for prison instead of college. How is a Black boy supposed to succeed even if he is latently talented? How can a 12-year-old like Tamir Rice achieve when he's shot dead by police officers at a park because they thought his toy gun was real?

Henry claimed that there is an unnecessary societal burden and illogical focus on *egalitarianism* in this country. To Henry and the many who share his views, egalitarian mindsets can only clog the process that has brought America to its pinnacle position in the world—the process of *elitism*. Elites find a way to rise, through talent, intelligence, hard work—whatever it may take—and deservedly hold their positions at the top, making society better for all.

If we are honest with ourselves, we can acknowledge that there is a disconcerting gap between the so-called process of elitism, which is arguably theoretical, and the real, lived experiences of millions of Americans. The comment made by the young woman in my class is valid and also representative of a widespread problem: Too many people today are judged unfairly, mistreated, or denied access to critical resources and opportunities because of biases about them. Many of these prejudices have historical and archaic roots but still persist today because, to an extent, these stereotypes have become normalized over time. The repetition of people-to-people injustices throughout history became aggregated, permeating through practice and serving to systematically keep people down and leave many behind. Structures like policy, meant to maintain *order* (think stop-and-frisk), may resemble vestiges from a more overtly oppressive former society, one with a narrower concept of whom order is supposed to be maintained *for*. This unfairness can be traced into today, with gaps in opportunity related to education, health, crime and punishment, employment, and many other factors that affect our ability to lead to happy and healthy lives.

Implicit or explicit biases should have no place in schools, where we must believe that children are capable of great things, even if some need more nurturing than others. So many future outcomes depend on what happens in school experiences. If pedagogy can better facilitate the process of self-discovery over self-denial, our communities would be more equipped to tackle the ever-growing social challenges we face. We could potentially tap into pools of latent but brilliant talent that is now going underutilized. Accessing this talent requires realizing that education is our greatest collective responsibility. Together, in and out of schools, we can always provide better support systems and opportunities for more of our students who currently fall behind. So while I somewhat agree with Henry's premise that the "measure of a just society" is found not in the proportionality of success of different groups but in the success of individuals, to me it is also found in how that society treats its most vulnerable populations.

A better measurement of a just society would be exhibited in the ability of that society to collectively uplift young people and empower them to work to improve the whole. The true strength of our institutions and our overall democracy is in the extent to which marginalized individuals and groups are able to transcend the limits of their background. My research project, though limited in scope, shows that when people are sufficiently helped—and let's be clear, through hand-*ups*, not hand-*outs*—their agency increases. When people become self-sufficient and can stand firmly on their own two feet, they may be likelier to make meaningful contributions back to society. Investing in people who will enlist in the goal to create a brighter future is an investment worth betting the house on.

After all, human life is fundamentally characterized by social interdependence. And inequality might be ripping apart our democratic fabric. The theory of "weak-link" economics says that an economic structure or ecosystem is only as strong and functional as its weakest component. Economists Chris Anderson and David Sally demonstrate this theory with the example of soccer as a "weak-link sport." Having a soccer team of moderately skilled players who make few mistakes has a higher likelihood of winning than does a team with one superstar and many lower-skilled players (Anderson & Sally, 2013).

If the United States wants to be more of a winner in the economic "World Cup," we should think deeply about this soccer analogy when considering how to treat education. We should shift our perspective to see that the opportunity gap is hurting all Americans. A McKinsey report showed that if the United States had narrowed identity-based educational divides in 1998, the national GDP could have increased by up to $525 per capita by 2008 (Auguste, Hancock, & Laboissière, 2009). Those various disparities, when viewed at the global level (between U.S. students and those across the world), may have deprived our economy of up to $2.3 trillion of economic output.

Furthering each student's potential is not a zero-sum game but a solution that is mutually beneficial for all. One person's success should open more doors of opportunity for others. Our educational system should thus foster the agency that all of our students have and take a stand against letting so many children fall through the cracks.

By simply attempting to learn what makes our students unique, we can identify more of their strengths and start to better recognize their inherent potential. As educator-philosopher Paulo Freire (1972) contended, students must learn to see school as a place to critically think about what limits them in life. This is likely what is meant by the (paraphrased) popular sentiment, "I am against letting schooling interfere with education," which is often credited to Mark Twain.[2]

Taking this idea to heart, I tend to give my undergrad students a break after midterms. Sometimes I'll put on a movie like the iconic *Stand and Deliver* (Musca & Menéndez, 1988). It is based on a true story about high school teacher Jaime Escalante, who decided to teach calculus in a failing school in East Los Angeles. He helped his students by first getting them to acknowledge their own history in order to better realize their agency. In the movie, Escalante tells them, "It was your ancestors, the Mayans, who first contemplated the zero. The absence of value. True story. You burros [donkeys] have math in your blood." Eventually, this radical approach helped Escalante get unprecedented numbers of students to pass the AP Calculus exam. The school board became suspicious of this achievement because the students who were passing the difficult exam for the first time did not fit the anticipated, and perhaps "White enough," profile. After multiple state-mandated retests, Escalante's students proved that they had indeed mastered calculus for themselves.

When a student owns her background, she develops a more powerful sense of agency and the essence of what it will take for her to succeed. Character is measured by much more than one's tenacity. Warmth, humility, charisma, inquisitiveness, attentiveness—these are just a few of the other qualities that we should look to nurture and reward. Rather than box our students into a preconceived notion of important values and qualities, we should allow them to impact society and leave their own mark on their own terms. Education is a lifelong process, and schools lay the strongest foundation for lifelong learning by placing students' well-being and dignity at the forefront of their priorities.

*

It's not a stretch to say that our lives may literally *depend* on treating education as our greatest collective responsibility. Not only do educational policies fail our children, but schools themselves are no longer physically safe. Today we are almost desensitized to the shootings that take place in our sacred educational spaces, from those at higher education institutions (like the spring 2019 shooting at the University of North Carolina at Charlotte) to those at elementary schools like Sandy Hook. It's an understatement to say that there is a heavy burden that all this senseless violence leaves us with.

Safety is a resource that I would argue we administer unevenly and think about illogically. Given that cases of mass violence are likelier to take place in more-affluent, predominantly White places, it makes little sense to me that schools that serve lower-income students of color continue to see a greater law enforcement presence. And in these schools, officers often discipline students for various minor offenses. Black and Latinx students make up 70% of in-school arrests, a pipeline that directly connects to our country having the largest incarceration rate in the world.

In 2015, I saw a viral video of a Black girl being violently thrown from her school desk and then arrested by an officer. In a short op-ed titled "Policing Schools and Dividing the Nation," I wrote that events such as this one are not only harmful to cohesive learning environments but also extremely detrimental to our overall social harmony. Harmony is the opposite of violence (Kundu, 2015). If we, rather than letting smaller disturbances (the student was reprimanded for not putting her cellphone away) be handled by teachers and school leadership, require law enforcement to resolve nonthreatening issues, our students are bound to feel distrust toward these instruments and their actors.

Social philosopher Louis Althusser (1971) labeled law enforcement as a necessary but Restrictive State Apparatus (RSA), one that maintains order through enforcing social sentiments and cultural cohesion. Our police can strengthen our social bonds by using force only when it is absolutely necessary, such as in the case of a school shooting. Instead, what we frequently see is that law enforcement performs a sharply contradictory function: It divides the public through a mismanagement of these critical responsibilities.

Why does this matter in the context of education?

Because while police overtly enforce the law, their unequal handling of authority is a function of a larger American ideological issue. That ideology is at stake in how we handle our education systems. Althusser labeled schools as the main Ideological State Apparatus (ISA) that is tasked with ironing out creases in the collective fabric by developing upright citizens. Our schools have the potential to mold the next generation to be both patriotic and keenly aware of social problems that must be addressed because schools nurture children who become our future engineers, teachers, doctors, and police officers.

If law enforcement is given unequal authority to take command in certain schools and not in others, they interfere with the functions of both RSA and ISA institutions. If a child is beaten and then arrested for using a cellphone in class, we have to ask, Is this serving to keep us safe and united? We can't blame the problem on either police or schools alone because the harmony of public institutions is what can stop such ruthless violence. Treating our schools and students as equally as possible, and treating education as our greatest collective responsibility, can work to keep our communities safe and intact.

Donald Trump called education the "civil rights issue of our time"[3] in his first congressional address, taking after Barack Obama, Arne Duncan, and George W. Bush. Yet a more applicable statement for the current crises in education might be words used to describe the urgency of civil rights by Martin Luther King Jr.: "We must learn to live together as brothers or perish together as fools" (King, 1965). These words ring powerful and are, to an extent, research backed. King urged us to accept the "inescapable network of mutuality" that makes up our communities (King, 2012).

It is beyond time for our schools to live up to our most fundamental democratic promises. There are certainly many debates worth having on topics that surround education—what to teach, how to teach, even when to teach—but the *who* and *why* should be obvious. Everyone deserves to be educated because everyone also benefits from that. The question, How much should we value the education of other people's children? has only one acceptable answer: As much as is humanly possible.

Introduction

From Seeing Roses in Concrete
to Believing Schools Are Gardens

At the end of the song "Mama's Just a Little Girl," the legendary Tupac Shakur raps the poem "The Rose That Grew from Concrete." The poem describes a rose that is tenacious enough, given its desire to reach the sun, to break through the concrete under which it was first a seed. Metaphorically, the whole song is about a young Black teenager who, despite experiencing trauma and abuse, endures her struggles and raises children. The words can be considered praise for the resilience of young, single parents from underresourced backgrounds who persevere through the toughest forms of adversity.[1] I recommend that all my readers take a small pause and listen to the poem or the whole song now.

There is an undeniable power to Tupac's simple message: This rose is extraordinary and beautiful. It deserves recognition for beating impossible odds and blossoming in such a harsh terrain. And instead of focusing our attention on the obviously damaged petals, we should realize—and celebrate—the flower's will to reach the sun.

When I first heard this poem everything else faded into the background. I didn't hear it in the song I mention but rather as background narration to a Powerade commercial during the 2015 NBA playoffs. The commercial starred former MVP Derrick Rose, who served as a personified reference to the rose that grew from concrete. The commercial showed Rose as a teen, riding his bike through the Chicago neighborhood of Englewood on the way to the United Center where he would go on to play for his hometown Chicago Bulls.

While listening to the poem, I had a flashback to driving through the neglected and broken-down streets of Chicago's South Side, including Englewood, during my undergrad days at the University of Chicago. Traveling those roads sometimes made me uneasy. Students were regularly discouraged from wandering into those starkly different neighborhoods that were worlds apart from our privileged university bubble, even though they were just a short distance from campus. Looking back, I realize that part of my nervousness was rooted in feeling a sense of "I don't belong or I'm not welcome here." It stands to reason that members of those left-behind communities might often rightfully feel the exact same thoughts toward the greater society that has denied them some of the most basic resources.

As the poem continued, I also remembered getting to watch Derrick Rose dominate at the United Center when my Portland Trail Blazers faced the Bulls. Near the end of the commercial the narrator says, "We are the roses, this is the concrete, these are my damaged petals," while a young Derrick Rose rides his bike through Chicago's South Side. The last lines in the ad, "Don't ask me why, ask me how," gave me chills. The sentiment resonated with me deeply. Coincidentally, it seemed to magically align with research I was just starting to develop on the topic of student achievement. I wanted to learn how students can overcome challenges and make it out of the concrete.

I wonder what Tupac would think of the commercialization of his work—not the general sharing of his art but rather the diffusion of his ideas in this way. For instance, the Powerade ad came with the hashtag #JustAKid—the moral being that *any* kid, from the South Side or the South Bronx, can rise from near nothing to achieve incredible things. Was that the point Tupac was trying to make—that with enough passion and persistence, and maybe even a little Powerade, success is possible for every child?

Advertisers have a knack for tapping into our value systems to make us buy stuff. In the case of the Powerade commercial, the message that individualism reigns supreme is a cultural value rooted deep within American identity. But the fact that the ad glossed over the concrete itself—environmental barriers to achievement and success—troubled me. If schools are gardens, a narrow focus on individualism may keep us from growing as many roses as possible. We may be amid plenty of rosebuds that need just a little extra fertilizer to bloom.

Though we'll never know for sure, I remain skeptical that Tupac was championing individual aptitude as the end-all-be-all for success. He explicitly calls out the concrete, a structure that held this flower and many others down while leaving permanent scars. Tupac encourages learning from this success story by asking *how* it was possible for this rose to bloom because, ideally, the answer will help other young people who face similar situations.

That is the point of this book: to consider that all young people are full of potential for growth, which we can see especially if we better understand the circumstances of their lives and how the concrete functions. In the chapters to come, I will share takeaways from my research on the academic and professional achievement of roses that are unique in their triumph but not unique in terms of their potential. For this research project, I specifically studied successful students of color from low-income backgrounds to learn how they increased their agency. I have worked to understand the larger processes at play by also questioning how individuals come to form certain goals in the first place. I was curious about how they learn the methods to obtain those goals and come to dedicate their efforts toward them.

James Clear (2018) tells us in his bestseller *Atomic Habits*, "Goals are about the results you want to achieve. Systems are about the processes that lead to those results" (p. 23). The book I have written is about better understanding those *systems* in the context of students who experience multiple challenges and obstacles. From my research participants, I have learned that high levels of success are possible for all students if their homes, institutions, and selves can provide or leverage the right supports and opportunities. The same should go for all people as they strive to reach the personal and professional benchmarks that matter to them in other arenas.

To heed Tupac's call, I wanted to start my research by simply asking, How? Essentially, I study students who beat the statistical predictions that they will fail. My goal is to learn how they succeed and to celebrate (not question) their stories by sharing them. How do roses that grow up in situations as tough as concrete learn to thrive? My main research question states this another way: How do students who are initially socially and economically disadvantaged explain what it takes to overcome significant obstacles and succeed? Working to find answers to this question is the central focus of my research and the premise of this book.

AMERICAN CONCRETE IS FORMIDABLE

Even though the United States holds a reputation for being a land of opportunity, a person's educational outcomes are still influenced by factors of race, class, and demography. Research in social science consistently shows that American students from wealthier backgrounds attain higher levels of education in their lives (Bowles & Gintis, 1976, 2011; Duncan & Murnane, 2014; Fruchter, Hester, Mokhtar, & Shahn, 2012). Furthermore, students with more economic advantages receive a higher-quality education and better cultural training on how to succeed in various situations and environments when they are older (Bourdieu & Passeron, 1977; Ransaw & Majors, 2016).

Disparities in educational quality and attainment are important because they directly affect the different possibilities individuals have for success: There is a direct correlation between the highest level of education a person possesses and the economic returns they can expect to receive over the course of their life (Brand & Xie, 2010; Roska, Grodsky, Arum, & Gamoran, 2007). When we separate groups by race, we find this correlation weaker for Black students than for White students, however. In a widely circulated study, economists Chetty, Hendren, Jones, and Porter (2018) examined intergenerational mobility—how much a child will earn compared to their parents—and found that educational opportunity had little impact on Black–White income gaps over time.

How, then, do we make sense of the students who *are* able to leverage educational opportunity to improve their economic condition? What factors in their experiences supported this success? Though differences in social mobility are commonly analyzed with large, aggregate data to understand trends, studying individual cases might better reveal how structural factors affect people and how they learn to maneuver around them. In a sense, this is why I encourage my students to give their own examples of the interpersonal so that we can personify these sometimes hard-to-envision social phenomena.

"Joe Hernandez" is one of the 50 individuals I profiled in my research. He provides one example that might help us better understand the complex relationship between social class and educational opportunity. Joe was born to a thirteen-year-old single mother and spent much of his early childhood homeless and struggling to survive. Throughout his early life, Joe and his mom constantly moved around New York City, often sleeping in city shelters, subway cars, and sometimes even in cardboard boxes. At one point, things were so bad that Joe was hospitalized for malnourishment. When Joe was twelve, his mom gave birth to his sister. At this point, with the burden of child care becoming too heavy to bear alone, Joe's mother reached out to her sister. Joe's aunt took him into her home in Edison, New Jersey, and this was a major turning point in his life.

Academically, the effects of this move were almost immediate. Joe had always been bright and curious but was behind a grade level in New York due to his challenging lifestyle. In Edison, equipped with a new support system in and out of school, Joe not only caught up but also achieved at higher levels. He met the greater expectations that were set for him by his teachers, peers, and mentors.

Throughout this book, I will use the word "support" to describe the various types of assistance that help students who have multiple needs and challenges succeed. In each case, the supports I describe will vary but will have some commonality as well. I define "support" in the following way: A support is any factor, whether it be a relationship, a tool, or a system, that implicitly or explicitly acknowledges a person's position of need and then subsequently eases that burden through specific, pinpointed help. Having a support means that a person does not simply have to rely on their own internal fortitude to reach their goals.

Outside of school, Joe particularly took notice that his new friends' parents placed a high value on their kids studying at home and participating in highly structured after-school activities. Joe started to internalize these lessons for himself because he realized that they must be important. He started to hold himself accountable and to mimic what he observed, which eventually led him to form stronger academic and professional goals. As a result, he started to see himself and his own potential in a new light.

Today, Joe is 23 years old. He recently graduated from an elite private college in the state of New York with a major in international business and a triple minor in philosophy, global studies, and economics. He is currently on a scholarship in the United Kingdom to get his master's degree in politics, governance, and public policy so that he can learn about education policy in Europe. He has hopes of eventually working to implement international best practices into the American educational system. We will revisit Joe's story later in this book to extract key elements that I hope will help more of our students get ahead no matter their specific situations.

Joe represents achieving the American Dream, a dream that for many other deserving students goes unrealized or, in the words of Langston Hughes (1959), becomes "a dream deferred" due to a lack of basic resources. Joe's level of academic and professional success—which in this book I will generally categorize as completing a bachelor's degree, entering into the professionalized workforce, or enrolling in a professionalized graduate school program—is a bar that we should believe all our students are capable of reaching.[2]

This "Sparknoted" version of Joe's story highlights how someone's demographic background—such as their neighborhood or household income level—can contribute to the overarching "achievement gap," the disparity in educational attainment and other academic outcomes between students of color from low-income backgrounds and their wealthier, White counterparts (Boykin & Noguera, 2011; Ladson-Billings, 2006; Reardon & Bischoff, 2011). Before moving to Edison, Joe grew up in one of New York City's poorest neighborhoods, where more than 80% of residents identify as Black or Latinx and only 10% of high school seniors graduate ready for college (Fruchter et al., 2012). By contrast, in the wealthiest neighborhoods of Manhattan fewer than 10% of residents identify as Black or Latinx, and the vast majority of students graduate from high school college-ready (Fruchter et al., 2012). Though these neighborhoods are often no more than 10 miles away from each other, they are clearly worlds apart.

In the United States, the differences in wealth and corresponding college readiness levels are also demonstrative of an underlying, mandated separation of people of color from well-resourced communities (i.e., Englewood, which is known as the "murder capital" of Chicago). Opportunities for social mobility largely remain more available in wealthier communities that typically have fewer minorities (Chetty, Hendren, Jones, & Porter, 2018; U.S. Census Bureau, n.d.). By moving to Edison, Joe found access to a stable home, to a good public school system, and to other social and cultural resources. The intersection of these different factors brought about one of the major turning points in his life. I have decided to structure this book in a similar order by organizing my findings by categories of home and family, social and school settings, and the ever-evolving human. I named the last category such to remind us that we are all constantly evolving products of our inheritances and environments, and so it also logically follows that none of our students are ever predetermined to fail.

By acknowledging these types of opportunities and their effects on students, some scholars argue that instead of an *achievement* gap (an idea that can reinforce the notion that achievement is determined solely by hard work and individual aptitude), America suffers from an *opportunity* gap. I place myself in this camp. The idea of an opportunity gap reinforces the notion that other disparities—income, wealth, and quality of life—play a role in limiting possibilities for success among children with fewer resources (Darling-Hammond, 2010; Kundu & Noguera, 2014; Milner, 2012). To put the opportunity gap into perspective, in 2017, 11% of White students were unable to get their high school diplomas on time. For Black, Latinx, and American Indian students, these rates were 22%, 20%, and 28% respectively (Annie E. Casey Foundation & Center for the Study of Social Policy, 2019). None of these outcomes are optimal, and our systems could improve for *all* students: Nationwide, about two-thirds of 8th-grade students were not at the proficient level for math in 2017, a figure that has not improved much since 2009.

Unfortunately, the schools and teachers who serve the students with the least resources often fend for themselves. They are expected to combat the complex myriad of factors that influence underachievement—many of which come from outside the classroom—without support from the larger community (Duncan & Murnane, 2014; Ladson-Billings, 2009; Noguera, 2003). For example, when Joe was a homeless student in New York City, he lacked basic nutrition, clothing, and shelter. It stands to reason that whether or not he realized it, on a daily basis he was dealing with immense levels of stress that no child should have to endure. While Joe's life improved when he moved to his aunt's suburb, many other students are unable to distance themselves from the daily constraints they face when their most basic needs go unmet.

And yet, despite the evidence that huge disadvantages continue to manifest through class and race, there are many overly simplistic explanations for what fosters social mobility. Many of these do not take into account privilege and race (Bonilla-Silva, 2010; Lewis, 2003). Instead, these theories are rooted in basic ideologies of meritocracy and individualism; their proponents argue that the United States is a postracial and "colorblind" state with equal access to ladders of opportunity for all who are willing to work hard enough to climb them (Henry, 1995; McWhorter, 2000).

A relatively recent example of an application of this logic is the Supreme Court case *Parents Involved in Community Schools v. Seattle School District*, in which it was ruled that school district policies that use race alone as a qualification for school assignment are unconstitutional. Though rhetorically these positions may carry some merit, similar to how we would all love to believe in a working and democratic elitism, what resulted was that the ruling effectively stopped the Seattle public schools's ability to desegregate nondiverse schools (Love, 2009). The basis for the ruling was that racial classifications present a kind of favoritism that is unconstitutional and discriminatory toward majority White groups.

Sociologist Eve Ewing (2018) urges us to remember that, similar to "an electrical current running through water, race has a way of filling space even as it remains invisible" (p. 10). A person's intent to be unbiased does not really matter so much when all of our systems and sets of systems are deeply embedded in patterns of structural inequality, "churning out different outcomes for different people in ways linked to race . . . with or without the consent, awareness or intentions of individuals" (p. 12). And though policy was more overtly racist in decades prior, we still feel its effects today. Like a "merry-go-round," Ewing says, "the machine is functioning with or without you" (p. 13).

And so our schools, through no fault of their own, are complicit in the processes of furthering and maintaining structural racism and structural inequality. They maintain this racism and inequality because they are the products of these systems—the way that neighborhood lines are structured and the resulting tax brackets for schools are created—directly becoming instruments of the status quo. When White soldiers returned from World War II, they were given housing vouchers in affluent suburbs; Black soldiers had no such safety net. The effects of these policies are directly felt today in the unequal school funding structures that separate good schools from bad ones by leveraging property values. It is unreasonable for us to ask schools and their constituents to change these massive, historic dynamics that affect them—at least not by themselves, without reciprocal help from us.

Fortunately, there is much we can do to ease some of these burdens. Given the complexity of the modern opportunity gap, one place to start is to simply hold equally rounded views on success—views that at least acknowledge the existence of racial and income-driven factors beneath the surface of meritocracy and individualism. Rugged individualism is a feel-good concept that does nothing to improve our current problems. When researchers account for the importance of both individual and social factors, we might be able to better understand the different obstacles that stand in the way of students' learning. Then we can be more equipped to address these different issues more effectively. We might be able to get more hands on deck, as other community members realize that they don't have to be in schools directly to lend a hand to the cause.

Let me take a moment to clarify something. I would never argue that possessing a strong individual work ethic is not a significant ingredient of success. After a lecture I once gave at Sinclair Community College in Ohio, a student asked me if I was against competition. Of course not, I replied. As much as possible, I am a proponent of *fair* competition. We should look to create conditions that allow students to better realize their potential, so they can strategically tap into their capacities and more effectively pursue what they want in life. Healthy competition improves the whole.

By reframing our longstanding beliefs and considering that obstacles at the social, economic, and racial levels do affect individual outcomes, we can figure out how to better facilitate achievement for students like Joe, who face large obstacles but are capable of thriving, competing, and contributing to society. By sharing examples and takeaways from real students who beat the odds, I will show that success can be viewed from a dynamic perspective. These examples are not to say that "because these people made it, anyone can," but rather, "look what is possible when we help our students in these ways." I will highlight the various types of systemic challenges that students face today and describe the forms of social and cultural supports that allow students to learn how to overcome these challenges.

By association, then, an underlying challenge of work such as mine is to make institutions and communities feel more accountable for the success of *all* students. I hope to make the argument that supporting the achievement of more students is a necessary investment in the livelihood of all. This book makes a modest case for raising our collective responsibilities as stakeholders in education, our greatest public promise, in an age of increased attention toward privatization and individualization. I hope that the power of stories can help us get there.

When some roses grow from concrete and others flourish in lush flower beds, we should realize that there are important roles that we can play as community members, stakeholders, and architects of the gardens. The earlier we step up to these challenges, the sooner we can learn how to grow together, rather than being forced to slowly wilt, apart.

OVERVIEW OF THE FOLLOWING CHAPTERS: CHOOSE YOUR OWN EXPERIENCE

I believe that life is about, or at least should be about, a quest for peace—peace with those whom we love, with those who surround us, and, maybe most importantly, peace with ourselves. Without the last, it seems relatively impossible to achieve the first two. That is the order in which I have structured this book. This structure provides a reflection on how some people find and are guided toward finding peace in these facets—within their home and family, within their social circles and communities, and internally, within themselves—that constitute their lives broadly.

As useful as I hope this text will be for students, it might also be interesting for people who are curious generally about the roles that identity, goals, relationships, and purpose play in life. In that regard, I wrote the book for a variety of audiences. Ideally, all readers will be able to gain new insights on the complexity of academic and professional achievement. At the same time, I realize that different people, depending on what hats they wear, will have different proclivities and will be drawn to content most relevant to them. I have organized the remaining chapters to make it easier for readers to get what they need most so that they can best meet their goals for picking up my project in the first place. Though the Table of Contents offers some direction, the following road map should provide more detailed guidance.

The Prologue (which you may have already read), the Introduction (which you are reading), and Chapter 1 are intended for all audiences, though they may be most appreciated by those who are interested in education. These sections lay out my main motivation for taking on this work: to challenge the notion that individualism is an omnipotent force that determines a person's success. Perhaps ironically, in describing the stories and achievements of a uniquely driven group of individuals, I will attempt to flip this notion, and these initial chapters lay the groundwork for me to do.

Chapter 1 is fairly academic, as I describe in more detail some popular perspectives on achievement in the United States. Here, I set the foundation I need to problematize these mainstream notions over the rest of the book. I also introduce the concept of "grit," my primary counterpoint to agency, to describe how the idea of grit can create an unintentional trap that ignores certain social elements of success. I make the argument that to more comprehensively understand the achievement gap, certain context is necessary. Arguing this point entails drawing upon some foundational scholarship in the field of urban education. But, rest assured, after getting a tad heavy with theory, I will conclude with a couple more lighthearted examples of why achieving success requires more than an individual's drive.

Chapter 2 may be the most theoretically dense chapter, perhaps most appealing to those who wish to gain a stronger scholarly foundation of the main concepts discussed in this work. In particular, I introduce the historical conceptualization of agency and address how agency can complement grit specifically by pinpointing where students are full of potential, rather than focusing on their supposed deficiencies. You will see how I hypothesize the functional relationship between agency and grit, which is observable through what scholars call a "conceptual framework." I present my working definition of "agency," which informed my academic research, in order to reach the findings I present here.

Chapters 3, 4, and 5 are again intended for broad audiences, specifically to provide readers with the crux of my research findings. These chapters are presented to be useful for learning how to foster the agency and grit of students in the environments that they inhabit every day. The chapters are presented in order of "The Home and Family," "The Social Environment and School Settings," and, finally, a look inward to "The Ever-Evolving Human." These chapters present vivid student narratives that help simplify the complexities of overcoming limitations that a person might inherit based on where they are born. I hope that the findings I draw from these stories, which focus on the role of supporting characters in each of the students' lives, are particularly useful for parents, practitioners, educators, policy influencers, and other stakeholders who care about influencing and improving the lives of young people.

I conclude with Chapter 6 to make the case that we cannot normalize failure. The people who are getting education right don't do that. Our most vulnerable students need us to first believe in them. By focusing on their strengths—the assets they bring to the table—we can work to counter any shortcomings they face. In this chapter, I describe how the findings I present can be applied to real-world settings and scenarios that increase the agency of all students. I will take you on a short field trip to visit two New York City high schools where I also take my undergraduate students so they can see learning in action. These schools are vibrant in their culture and unwavering in their mission to support youth. They demonstrate simple strategies that can help other communities do the same.

In the Appendix, the reader will find materials for a more "under the hood" look at my research design and methodology. I will describe how I recruited and selected my participants and the interviewing methods and protocol I used, among other considerations, such as the limitations of my project. I start this section by discussing why I got into research and my hopes for using research for good. The Appendix will also include a rationale for why qualitative methods are well suited for answering my main questions.

In the various journeys we embark on to achieve our goals, we learn not only our limits but also what we are capable of. So, it may actually be obvious that the quest for peace is not necessarily peaceful. It requires dedication, determination, and a healthy dose of confronting reality. The quest for peace requires that at times we collectively take a stand for what we believe in. There will always be times that test us and require us to rely on one another. And to rely on one another, we must seek to find and bring out the best in one another, supporting all of our dreams so they are no longer deferred.

I hope you feel free to read this book it its entirety. The agency to do so is yours.

CHAPTER 1

Rugged Individualism and the Co-option of Grit

The United States has long celebrated "rugged individualism" as a cultural value linked to excellence. The phrase can be traced to Herbert Hoover (1934), who is often credited for coining the term in his book *The Challenge to Liberty*:

> It has been used by American leaders for over a half-century in eulogy of those God-fearing men and women of honesty whose stamina and character and fearless assertion of rights led them to make their own way in life. (pp. 54–55)

The concept of rugged individualism implies that individual effort is the key to determining one's future. Consistent with this logic is a modern wave of psychology referred to as "positive psychology." Positive psychology identifies behaviors such as self-affirmation, mindset, and, especially, grit as the main components to achievement (Duckworth & Gross, 2014; Duckworth, Peterson, Matthews, & Kelly, 2007; Duckworth, White, Matteucci, Shearer, & Gross, 2016; Dweck, 2008).

"Grit" has meant many things over the years. In the 1930s, *Grit* was a well-read weekly family magazine around the rural United States. *True Grit* was a popular Western film in 1969 and was remade in 2010, starring Jeff Bridges. And for as long as anyone can remember, grits have been a Southern breakfast staple (one that I like with grilled shrimp and the occasional mimosa). But today, the quality of "grit" is widely defined as tenacity, akin to that quality of rugged individualism that we have come to so admire.

The term seems to be woven into the fabric of Americanism. In Barack Obama's 2017 farewell address in Chicago, he got emotional when he mentioned his wife, Michelle. "You took on a role you didn't ask for," he said. "And you made it your own with *grace and with grit* and with style, and good humor" (Obama, 2017). Grit in all its forms has come to represent the American character, hearty and resilient.

Angela Duckworth, the preeminent global scholar of grit, established the validity of the concept in creating unwavering persistence for long-term goals (Duckworth et al., 2007). Particularly interested in the achievement of children, Duckworth describes grit to be an observable trait that successful students embody. She has also convincingly shown through many large samples that grit can predict professional success in adults (Duckworth, 2016; Duckworth & Gross, 2014; Duckworth et al., 2007).

Duckworth's theory defines "grit" as a behavior that allows people to stay focused on their long-term goals, undeterred by immediate setbacks (Duckworth, 2016; Duckworth et al., 2007). Grit can also predict a person's proclivity for having good mental health and sense of well-being (Duckworth et al., 2007; Lucas, Gratch, Cheng, & Marsella, 2015; Vainio & Daukantaitė, 2016). Grit can be thought of, in lay terms, as the day-in and day-out hard work necessary for achieving one's big-picture goals. Duckworth has often described grit as a person's North Star. Through her research, she demonstrates that a "gritty" person will persist even in the most drastic circumstances. For example, in research she conducted at West Point, Duckworth found that the cadets who scored higher on a self-report grit scale were more likely to endure "Beast Barracks," the grueling training regimen students must complete to stay in good standing in their first year at the elite military academy (Duckworth et al., 2007).

Some writers have used the grit framework to make the additional claim that noncognitive traits, like grit and strong-willed character, can hugely help (or are the most important quality in) students who are born and raised with personal and structural disadvantages. A notable example is Paul Tough's (2012) best seller, *How Children Succeed: Grit, Curiosity, and the Hidden Power of Character*. Tough's (2016) sequel, *Helping Children Succeed,* makes similarly attractive arguments to help address disparities in achievement.

However, as a result of grit research and its prominence, there seems to be a newly increased focus on individual attributes in conversations about education. Character-trait-based explanations for achievement have, for quite some time, spread into research about social mobility and academic achievement (Bidwell & Friedkin, 1988). Yet, while psychological studies support the idea that certain personality traits can lead to positive goal-setting and outcomes, these studies rarely consider the immeasurable impacts of structural factors in people's lives, such as poor housing conditions, limited access to healthy food options, or a general lack of certain social networks.

It's not necessarily a psychologist's job to have to think about these factors, but as a sociologist, I can't understand how we can afford to leave out these considerations when thinking about what children need to thrive. I suppose Duckworth agrees with this premise; she has become a very close mentor to me over the last few years and served on my dissertation committee so that we could push this dialogue further. One of my more humbling moments was hearing Duckworth praise my work as helping her understand how the grit narrative could be misused to hurt certain students (Mahnken, 2018).

For students like Joe Hernandez, whom I discussed in the Introduction and whose move to Edison, New Jersey, changed the course of his life, the poverty he had experienced mattered more than a little. The concept of grit does not adequately encompass or fully explain what helped Joe overcome the various setbacks he encountered as a boy. We desperately need richer context in educational research to better understand how students like Joe can someday be able to break cycles of intergenerational poverty.

The participants in the research described in this book should not be thought of as *exceptions* but rather as *exceptional*. They are not exceptions to any rules because the rules that were originally holding them down should be abolished. Similarly, in this book, the term "disadvantage" is not meant to be used in a derogatory or even a sympathetic manner but rather as a simple admission of the fact that some students in the American educational system are less privileged than others. As such, my participants are also representatives of possibility for all students.

INDIVIDUAL OUTCOMES ARE LARGELY PRODUCTS OF "SOCIAL AND CULTURAL REPRODUCTION"

The Coleman Report of 1966 was commissioned by the Department of Education and became a decade-long report that was historically influential (Coleman et al., 1966). The report showed that the school a child attends is actually less influential than the student's background and socioeconomic status. Since this landmark study, education research has continuously and unfortunately confirmed that high school students' demographic characteristics—specifically their race, home zip code, and family income levels—are still some of the most dominant predictors of their college-readiness levels (Blankstein, Noguera, & Kelly, 2016; Duncan & Murnane, 2014; Fruchter et al., 2012; Sharkey, 2013). This research starkly discredits the idea of elitism; sometimes the things that students "bring" from outside of school when they show up to learn are too formidable for a school and its staff to confront alone.

Neo-Marxians—those who believe in the ongoing and inevitable class struggles in capitalist societies—study education to show that schools and students are more influenced by the communities and class structure they live in than vice versa; this wave of scholarship finds that within the United States' economic system, schools are actually implicated in reproducing the class structure and maintaining the status quo by keeping social systems in place (Althusser, 1971; Bourdieu, 1974; Bowles & Gintis, 2011; Giroux, 1983). When I first started grappling with this idea, it felt like having a mini existential crisis. I had been interested in education for most of my adult life and saw it as a necessary and preventive resource for promoting social good. I, too, had been inculcated by the mainstream notion that schools provide ladders to economic opportunity for all, and now I was being forced to ask, So schools can actually make inequality worse?

This neo-Marxian position is often referred to as the "social and cultural reproduction" perspective of education and, on a deeper level, works as follows: Each generation transmits to the next one certain activities and forms of capital (economic, social, and cultural) that are rewarded at different levels by society and function in the perpetuation of social inequality (Bourdieu & Passeron, 1990; Coleman, 2000; Doob, 2015). Though economic capital (money and wealth) can be easier to spot and can even transfer from one group to another, social and cultural capital (relationships, norms, and customs) are more latently passed on but have incredibly important effects. Just think, out of the various jobs you may have held in your life, how many of them have been the result of having a connection that helped to get your foot in the door?

Social capital is comprised of relationships between group members, manifesting through shared understanding of social norms and pooled resources that are mutually beneficial. Social capital can also be thought of as access to different social networks and the benefits derived from participation in those networks (e.g., information and support; Kundu, 2019). Cultural capital is defined as nonfinancial assets that promote a person's social mobility beyond economic means. Cultural capital can be thought of as using one's symbolic toolbox and knowing how to (consciously and subconsciously) use language and behavior in different, complex social settings (Swidler, 1986). These are the main definitions of economic, social, and cultural capital that I used in my research.

I often tell students to think of social capital as the connections that can get you into the annual Met Gala, whereas cultural capital is knowing how to conduct yourself when you are there. I will go into more depth about these two concepts at the beginning of Chapter 4, "The Social Environment and School Settings," but it is important to have a baseline of knowledge on this subject to understand how schools, mentors, and other environmental factors can help students learn to gain social and cultural capital and to successfully navigate the pathways of becoming upwardly mobile.

These hidden reward systems make forms of structural privilege and disadvantage harder to notice and identify. The mechanisms that go into acquiring these different forms of capital often take place throughout all of one's schooling experiences, where certain codes, norms, expectations, and values are taught and learned. Depending on the school (or even the classroom) that children attend, they may be implicitly ushered toward higher and better educational tracks based on this "hidden curriculum" and their ability to regurgitate it (Jackson, 1990). These processes compound and continue into the job market, where more privileged applicants are more likely to receive opportunities, perhaps due to networks or various cultural cues and signaling.

The value of one's education is also largely determined by corresponding economic returns. Better schools, funded by local taxes, are typically found in wealthier neighborhoods and tend to have better facilities, food, equipment, and teachers. More advanced educational credentials, such as undergraduate and graduate degrees from "elite" institutions, often come with high tuition fees and other associated costs. Furthermore, the time commitments required to earn these degrees can impede one's ability to hold down a job. These factors make advanced degrees more exclusive to members of the upper class who can afford their ticket price or provide the credentials necessary to secure grants and loans (Bourdieu & Passeron, 1990; Collins, 2002; Khan, 2012).

These discrepancies play a large role in a person's expected career opportunities. A study shows that 6.5 million U.S. jobs, including frontline supervisors and hospitality managers, recently started requiring a college degree (Fuller & Raman, 2017). Many middle-class jobs have transitioned toward requiring a bachelor's degree. However, in the bottom 40% income bracket, only about one out of ten 25-year-olds have such a degree, which implies that only 10% of students in lower income brackets have a shot at landing a middle-class, family-sustaining job and improving their economic standing (Symonds, Schwartz, & Ferguson, 2011). These numbers provide an example of how educational attainment can stabilize and reproduce the existing social order (Johnson, 2014; Marsh, 2011).

Research that addresses individual traits and aptitudes needs to be rounded out with research that addresses the complex social contexts in which individuals live and operate. Neither type of research is sufficient to stand on its own to explain a person's achievement. Education research that focuses on success can benefit from concepts in sociology and psychology to comprehensively address the challenges of and workarounds for opportunity gaps. Theories around capital, social structures, and human agency seem important to include in discussions about what it takes to obtain a solid educational foundation to then increase one's economic mobility. It is also important to recognize that strict "functionalism"—the idea that there is no room for an individual's agency to successfully navigate within these systems—is also quite flawed. I will provide many examples of individuals who were able to climb, or "jump," into different (and sometimes more elite) social networks through learning how to leverage available resources and knowing where and how to look for help when needed. I will make the case that knowing how to use this type of *social* acuity is an integral component of an individual's agency. We should be actively teaching kids how to best ask for help and when it's most appropriate and beneficial to seek support.

The most well-suited answers for how students can effectively navigate various obstacles to success may lie somewhere between sociology and psychology, but the pursuit of these answers does not require a complicated theoretical framing. We can find a balance between the two ends of the sociology–psychology spectrum with an approach to the opportunity gap that reflects the complexity of the individual human experience, while acknowledging and supporting educational stakeholders.

SWIM TESTS AND AFRO-PUFFS

For an article in *The Players' Tribune*, former NBA superstar David Robinson (2016) wrote a "Letter to My Younger Self," in which he says, "Grit alone is not going to save you from sinking." He is writing to himself three decades before, at a time when he attempted his first Navy swim test, a daunting feat that requires 20 minutes of nonstop treading in the ocean followed by a series of laps. Robinson was built like a tank and could feel himself sinking like one during the test. His muscles burned out and he had to call it quits.

The following night as he lay awake in his bunk, young Robinson questioned his motivation for having joined the Naval Academy. Both his father and grandfather had been in the military. Following their service, both men worked tirelessly to provide for their families.

Robinson writes in the letter to his younger self that these role models worked hard to instill strong values in their children. They set examples that were worth following by being active mentors. He recalls that his father quizzed him each night on spelling different words from entire pages of the dictionary. He not only had to learn to spell words like "ambidextrous" but also had to learn what they meant.

Maybe it was this discipline that drove Robinson to excel at academics and to major in math in college. In his letter, Robinson assures his younger self that he does later pass the swim test. And it's not only that—upon graduating from the academy, he will make $1,200 a month as an ensign in the Navy. But there is more.

Due to his undeniable talent, he will go on to be the #1 draft pick by the San Antonio Spurs to play professional basketball and will make millions. He'll be nicknamed "The Admiral" because of his military service and will have a Hall of Fame career. He will be selected as an NBA All-Star 10 times, win two NBA Championships, receive an MVP Award, and bring home two gold medals as a member of the famed Dream Team. To this day, he remains the only NBA player to come from the Navy.

In the letter, Robinson advises his younger self to stay humble and not let these accolades go to his head. He writes that he should lead a modest lifestyle and use his new resources to give back to his community, so other youngsters can follow their dreams, too. He deduces that his salary as an ensign should be more than enough to support him, even when making NBA money, to truly become a self-sufficient young man.

The message in this time-capsule letter to himself is contained in these lines: "When you fail the swim test, don't get too bent out of shape. Just remember how your father built up your vocabulary with that thick dictionary . . . and when you get that signing bonus, don't start thinking about all the things you can do with $1 million. Instead, think about all the things your grandfather did with $100. And perhaps even more importantly, remember to always ask yourself, 'Why am I doing this?'"

Robinson asks his younger self to remember his identity, where he comes from, and his purpose in life because those are the most important things. He knows that humility and heritage are just as powerful as grit in making the biggest of dreams come true.

On the surface, it might not seem like the legendary pro athlete David Robinson shares much in common with 14-year-old Nathalie McGriff. Yet their stories are similar in key ways. Nathalie is the author of the comic book *The Adventures of Moxie McGriff*, the tale of a young girl who realizes that her "afro-puffs" contain magical powers capable of stopping vile monsters.

Nathalie, like her character Moxie, was once embarrassed about her natural hair and its texture. She told her mom, Angela Dixon, that she wanted it straightened because everybody else seemed to have straight hair. Dixon realized she had a chance to teach her daughter a valuable lesson about self-love. To turn the idea of normative beauty on its head, the two devised a plan to create the heroic Moxie Girl. And as an expression of defiance, Moxie's hair would be the source of her powers. I once asked Dixon if she'd be willing to talk to me about this journey. We had a pleasant chat (separate from my research design) in which she mentioned the following:

I felt sad because I remember growing up feeling the same way. Now, loving my hair, I wanted Nathalie to love herself too. It wasn't until after I had her that I started feeling secure in my Blackness and my Black Girl Magic. I wanted her to live her whole life secure, and so I decided to flip it. She hated to read, and I wanted to merge the two.

Dixon used this experience not only to bond with her daughter but also to embolden Nathalie's self-esteem through self-embrace. Coming from a community-organizer background, Dixon had the idea to enroll as a "mommy and daughter" team at a local crowdfunding contest in Jacksonville. There, the two won over $16,000 to publish their story.

Today, the dynamic duo continues to present Moxie Girl throughout the country, spreading their message about the power of self-acceptance to people of all ages. Nathalie's worldview has continued to grow as she fosters passion for reading and writing, and also for entrepreneurship. Dixon says:

I think she's learning that hard work pays off. In order for her to write a good book, she needs to read more books so that she can learn words, because no one wants to read the same words over and over again. I'm learning that it's good to spend quality time with your child. I'm learning how to be a better mom.

Similar to David Robinson's father, who taught David the word "ambidextrous," Angela is making sure that Nathalie's vocabulary expands through her own process. Nathalie recently learned how to spell and define "accentuate." This story goes to show how self-awareness and self-esteem can transcend wealth when it comes to setting kids up to succeed in life. Parent involvement, which I will address more thoroughly in Chapter 3, is one of the most important factors in helping children develop lifelong tools for achieving great things.

But how else is the story of Nathalie and Moxie Girl similar to that of David Robinson's swim test? In a sense, they are both testaments to harnessing the power of *human agency*—or the specific capacity that individuals have to enact free will to influence their lives and to achieve great feats. These two individuals were able to take a perceived flaw and work on retooling their existing impressions of themselves and their capabilities to eventually overcome the specific struggle they were facing.

Nathalie McGriff and David Robinson used self-reflection and critical thinking to achieve goals they desired and to find purpose and fulfillment along the way. Their goals ranged from developing superpowers and defeating book-eating monsters to staying afloat in the ocean for the most grueling of physical feats. Importantly, these stories highlight that educational experiences do not need to occur within school walls or be assessed through standardized measures to determine someone's aptitude. These stories are also a testament to the fact that learning is a lifelong process, and they lead me to the following questions: When the long-term payoffs of agency seem to be so high, what if fostering agency became a greater focus in schools, communities, and in other educational settings? What would that look like?

To answer these questions, we should first explore what "agency" truly means. We can start by revisiting grit (and ideas around effort) and considering what the concept of grit is lacking. After all, as we have discussed, social and cultural reproduction is a real phenomenon that stands in the way of total equality of opportunity. One of the main distinctions between agency and grit is this: Agency requires social and cultural context because it depends on the resources a person has at their disposal that affect their ability to achieve. Grit is primarily about a person's ability to follow their passion through intense perseverance despite obstacles. The concept of grit has been missing some sensitivity to the obstacles that specifically relate to structural forces. At the same time, the concept of agency could benefit from being less theoretical in nature and more action oriented. Through this give-and-take, it can start to become clearer how focusing on supporting the complementary nature of agency and grit might help more students, especially those who face the largest obstacles, learn to achieve great things.

GETTING TO AGENCY:
LIMITATIONS OF GRIT IN FULLY EXPLAINING ACHIEVEMENT

School districts have increasingly focused on character traits such as grit, self-control, and growth mindset to determine how they might affect things like attendance and testing ability (West et al., 2016). There is also growing interest in including these kinds of "noncognitive" factors in large assessments such as the National Assessment of Educational Progress (NAEP) and the Programme for International Student Assessment (PISA; Baker & O'Neil, 2016; Kwon, 2017; Zernike, 2016). These tests are highly regarded as "report cards" for student progress and comparison.

People are also interested in learning how grit may be *environmental*, or influenced by one's social factors. Newer research is looking at interventions that are designed to help foster grit in students, specifically in those who come from disadvantaged backgrounds (Shechtman, DeBarger, Dornsife, Rosier, & Yarnall, 2013). This is also a primary focus of mine, as I investigate it from a case-by-case basis.

Because of the pro-grit movement, it is important to realize that applying grit too widely in education could have potentially negative implications. There can be unintended consequences from overemphasizing individual traits as key to academic success. For one, as mentioned earlier, stressing individualism may mean ignoring educational disparities that are the result of privileges and disadvantages. In a system focused on individual traits, if children fail to live up to their potential, one might be inclined to think that they underachieve because they lack grit or motivation or, worse, because they have other inherent deficiencies, such as an apathetic attitude toward education (McWhorter, 2000).

Yet again, we know that certain determining factors of achievement lie outside of the student altogether. Interestingly, actual grit research does not pretend that grit by itself explains the complexity of how a student learns to achieve. Angela Duckworth (2016) says, "Of course, your opportunities— for example, having a great coach or teacher—matter tremendously, too, and maybe more than anything about the individual" (p. 42), and "I can tell you with complete conviction that every human trait is influenced by both genes and experience" (p. 79).

Yet, as grit continues to be sweepingly applied in school contexts, it becomes almost co-opted in a sense that Duckworth never intended. Fortunately, it *is* possible to expand upon grit—by adding to it a *social* perspective—to more adequately address how people form goals, navigate obstacles and challenges, and continue to improve their skills, competencies, and confidence over the course of their lives.

From a sociological standpoint, there are three important elements that are absent from the theory of grit, which keep grit from explaining how students really succeed: (a) Grit does not generally address the social contexts or structural challenges of the young people whose achievements it assesses; (b) grit is not necessarily rooted in a *dynamic* understanding of students' cultures, which constantly change and adapt under different environmental contexts; and (c) grit is not typically attentive to the important roles of social and cultural capital in students' lives.

Agency is one of the few concepts that can directly address these particular issues and complement grit. I will go in depth about the symbiosis of agency and grit and will explain how understanding this dynamic can be used to improve outcomes for all students.

CONCEPTUAL FRAMEWORK

There are some subquestions that logically follow my main research question: *How do students who are initially socially and economically disadvantaged explain what it takes to overcome significant obstacles and succeed?* These secondary questions get at the underlying character traits and qualities that are involved in success:

- What factors foster help-seeking behavior, allowing young people to develop their own networks and social support systems?
- What factors influence young people's positive attitudes about themselves and how they value education? What develops their motivations toward certain goals?
- How do young people describe themselves, and what traits seem associated with grit and/or agency?

I kept these questions as an undercurrent to my work to uncover both the social-level and the individual-level factors that play a role in a person's achievement. I did extensive background research on the conditions for student achievement, which led me to form the following hypothesis: Agency and grit influence each other in various ways and conjointly promote a person's academic and professional success. These two qualities are similar, and each one is critical to achieving goals; however, to make a contribution to the extensive literature on both subjects, I needed to clearly differentiate between agency and grit, to better understand how, when, and why they showed up in the stories that my research participants told.

On the most fundamental and surface level, there are some important distinctions between grit and agency: Grit is based on an individual's long-term goals and adherence to them; agency specifically revolves around a person's *position* in their social world, largely related to their socioeconomic status and ability to navigate constructs of power. I created a Venn diagram describing the most important components in each concept, to represent how these concepts are similar yet distinct (see Figure 1.1).

My research indicates that agency and grit can exist in a fluid dynamic that centers around how people form and achieve their goals through deliberate action; either quality can instigate or catalyze the development of the other. Agency and grit are mutually beneficial and especially so if someone is provided the right support systems and healthy environments they need to thrive. Agency, if supported by social and cultural resources, can allow someone to form specific goals as they start to see themselves in a new and improved light. Grit is the mechanism or tool used to help a person stay focused and on track. On the flip side, initial grit based on an existing interest can spur a person's goal formation and subsequent agency to keep climbing, through the same social and cultural resources. I have illustrated these pathways in Figures 1.2 and 1.3 to make this idea a little clearer.

Figures 1.2 and 1.3 show how grit and agency can influence one another, as well as how they may be codependent. Both concepts are involved in a person's goal formation and goal achievement. Through my work, I have learned that it can be incredibly important to recognize any seeds of interest

Figure 1.1. Agency and Grit: Commonalities and Distinctions

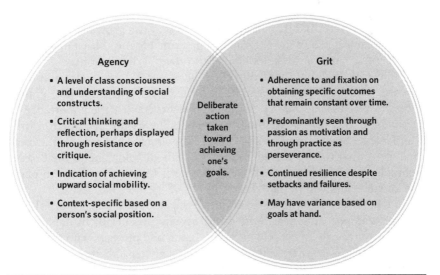

Agency

- A level of class consciousness and understanding of social constructs.

- Critical thinking and reflection, perhaps displayed through resistance or critique.

- Indication of achieving upward social mobility.

- Context-specific based on a person's social position.

Deliberate action taken toward achieving one's goals.

Grit

- Adherence to and fixation on obtaining specific outcomes that remain constant over time.

- Predominantly seen through passion as motivation and through practice as perseverance.

- Continued resilience despite setbacks and failures.

- May have variance based on goals at hand.

Figure 1.2. Initial Agency Leading to Success Through Grit as a Vehicle

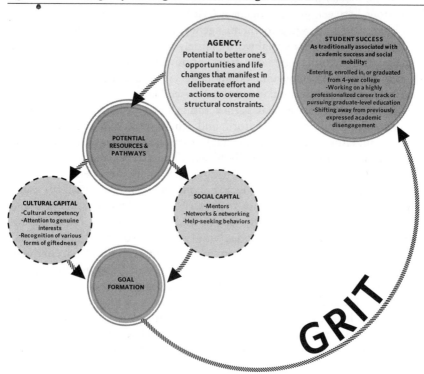

a student may have, and then nurture them so they can grow in the direction of their dreams. Each of my participants described to me at least one formative experience in their lives, to which this process could be traced.

"Imperial," whom I will introduce in Chapter 3, is one example of someone who had initial agency that turned into grit. Imperial's grandmother fostered his agency by helping him to first realize the importance of his potential as a Bronx community member. She used that pride to instill in him a level of commitment and obligation, which developed into professional goals that were centered around his sense of belonging to the Bronx. Eventually these feelings turned into a deep grit for improving urban planning and development in the Bronx.

In Chapter 3, we will see an example of the opposite trajectory. I will describe examples of how grit can lead to agency, specifically through social capital resources. "Gouvia" and "Sunny" each had mothers who displayed a level of grit toward their schooling, which they were able to instill in their children. This eventually led to their forming of specific academic goals and developing a continued agency that drove them to succeed.

Figure 1.3. Initial Grit Leading to Success Through Agency as a Vehicle

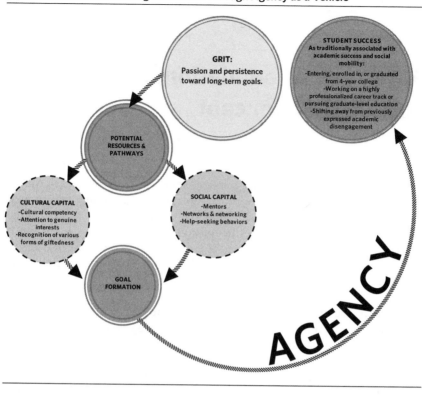

The dynamic between agency and grit will benefit from deeper investigation through a variety of methodological approaches. I tend to prefer approaches in research that give students a chance to record their own experiences and outcomes over time. Neither grit nor agency appear in one single way; both are largely qualitative as well, influenced by different factors and manifesting outwardly in different ways. The interchangeable relationship that I describe is by no means axiomatic; rather, the diagrams in Figures 1.2 and 1.3 can serve as a signpost for how one might monitor a student's progression toward self-actualization and goals.

CHAPTER 2

Agency as a Foundational Sociological Concept

People are dealt different hands at birth; some start life on a path that is more favorable for success than others do. This simple statement, though perhaps obvious to some, has brought the topic of human *agency* to the forefront of the most classical dilemma in all of sociology: How much influence do people truly have over their own lives? Sociologists have long wondered and studied the question of whether the impact of social structures has more power than human agency in determining outcomes of individuals.

"Social structures" refer to groups of institutions through which humans operate and interact with one another. Through their functions (such as laws that are enacted by courts), they can either propel or limit the opportunities that are available to certain populations. Structures are made up of the following: economic systems, described as class or income levels; institutions, such as schools, jails, or hospitals; and the relationships between large groups that are mandated formally through legislation, like tax brackets, which are determined by income (Barker, 2003). Social structures are all around us, guiding some of the most basic functions of everyday life.

Conceptually, we can think of structures existing at the systems level, in aggregated forms of individual experiences. Their architects are people with high amounts of power, such as a president; however, these people still generally require the compliance and approval of the larger populace, to remain in their posts.

Agency, on the other hand, refers to the extent to which individuals can use total free will to make the choices that affect them, given the existence of these ubiquitous social structures. It is a person's capacity to leverage resources to navigate obstacles and create positive change in their life. I will thoroughly define "agency" at the end of this chapter, hopefully in a way that allows it to be more identifiable in the real-life contexts of students, such as my participants, whom I will continue to introduce, and anyone else who is striving to improve the conditions of their life.

A CLASSIC SOCIOLOGICAL DEBATE AND FINDING
A BALANCE THROUGH GRIT AND AGENCY

In academic theory and research, structures and agency are typically characterized as having an antagonistic relationship, with one pitted against the
other. Those who hold strong structural perspectives often share a kind of
determinism, or a sense that individuals' lives are largely predetermined or
fated by the circumstances of their birth. From this perspective, agency is
downplayed and seen as having little utility in the face of the broad, powerful systems that can shape and even constrain human lives.

Alternatively, as we have discussed, there are theories that emphasize
notions of individualism, often through a belief in meritocracy—akin to
the idea of the rugged individual pulling themselves up by the bootstraps.
These arguments contend that people can generally chart their own course,
depending on how much work they put in, rejecting determinism and also
discounting structures to an extent. Scholars, politicians, and practitioners
who espouse this perspective seem attracted to the concept of grit and sometimes stretch it beyond Duckworth's intended scope to attribute the failure
of underachieving students to their own lack of tenacity. They also over-
simplify agency because agency implies the existence of structures and their
impacts on people's lives.

Though the agency–structure polarization sparks interesting theoretical discussions, the either–or divide is unhelpful to those who want to understand how social mobility works and how individuals learn to navigate
systems. Instead, investigating the intersections between the possibilities of
agency and the limits of structural conditions can contribute to studying
achievement and life trajectory. Most importantly, this could help identify
practical ways to support success pathways for more students.

In terms of educational contexts and teaching students, the influential
sociologist and cultural critic Henry Giroux (1983) stated:

> Central to the development of a radical pedagogy is a reformulation of this
> dualism between agency and structure, a reformulation that can make possible
> a critical interrogation of how human beings come together within historically
> specific social sites such as schools in order to both make and reproduce the
> conditions of their existence. (p. 13)

An underlying point of this book is to give more attention to the du-
alism between structure and agency that allows educational contexts to
better facilitate student achievement by acknowledging important realities,
especially for those students with less privilege. Giroux indicates that refor-
mulating these perspectives can foster an important, "radical" pedagogy,
in that it goes against the traditional sorting functions of schools, to help
marginalized students rise above obstacles.

The same notion is aligned with the foundational education work of philosopher Paulo Freire, which contends that unlocking the potential within students who are marginalized requires an explicit acknowledgment of factors that are oppressing them (Freire, 1968/1972). Freirean philosophy implies that if less-advantaged students could be taught to think critically about how structures impact their lives, they might learn to better strategize how to succeed despite the limitations of social origin.

A more modern example of this philosophy can be found within a correctional facility in Soledad, California, where Riche Edmond-Vargas and Charles Berry developed a curriculum to educate incarcerated men about the concept of "toxic masculinity." Through Success Stories, a nonprofit organization they founded in 2012, Edmond-Vargas and Berry, both formerly incarcerated, introduce feminist authors like bell hooks to prison groups and discuss with them the harmful effects of patriarchy on their own lives in inner cities (Nonko, 2019). Giving these men a space to confront topics like the objectification of women can be considered a *radical* pedagogy that is based around working against the deeply rooted masculine culture. The curriculum also empowers the adult students by equipping them to take their newly developing tools and language back to their community. There, they have the ability to potentially work with community members and to generate a social agency that can lead to positive change.

If we pay closer attention to the ways in which structure and agency complement and influence one another, we can eventually create tailor-made strategies to fix broken aspects of our communities and adopt more balanced perspectives that allow us to bridge theory and practice. In doing so, we acknowledge that structures do affect human behavior, whether consciously or not, and that *organized* human behavior can also enact structural change over time (Bourdieu & Passeron, 1977, 1990; Hurrelmann, 1988). That middle ground provides the platform to consider possibilities for positive social change. This is a perspective that seemingly integrates concepts such as grit by acknowledging that effort, perseverance, and passion are important in a person's success. At the same time, this view incorporates the reality that background matters a great deal because there is an entire ecosystem made up of social groups with varying amounts of power that can either propel or inhibit a person's abilities (Bronfenbrenner, 2009).

To bridge structure and agency pragmatically, my research has used grit and agency together to establish how both concepts are valid and to provide examples of how they might coexist so that we can recognize them in real life. Unlike much existing psychological research on grit, I have examined the concept through *sociological* methods and perspectives; uniquely, I also have focused on the achievement of low-income students of color who face a variety of challenges, which, again, effort cannot necessarily trump by itself. Most of all, I reject the notion that some students, the ones similar to the participants featured in this book, do not have grit simply because they do not exhibit the type of grit for which we are accustomed to look.

Furthermore, what I find interesting within this foundational sociological debate is that the *agency* side of the argument—the one that believes individuals can eventually ascend over the structural obstacles in their way—implies the existence of grit. The agency side is the one that makes room for us to realize that individual competencies are necessary (though not the be-all and end-all) for overcoming the limits someone can inherit at birth. So, fundamentally, agency and grit are *not* at odds with one another but are complementary. The structure side of the debate is the one that says individuals lack the complete power to ever become fully socially mobile.

I contend that having agency helps a person to initially visualize and care about certain goals, which is the first step in being able to achieve them. Individuals must be able to see goals as both personally significant and within the realm of possibility. Then they can develop strategies for attaining them. In this case, grit only starts to get introduced in the actual accomplishment of the goal. I will show that this initial visualization of goals often benefits from social support that takes into account a person and their experiences.

In school settings, students are more likely to be engaged in classrooms with teachers whose approach they enjoy because they are better able to connect with the material. This example indicates that some teachers might help their students display more of their inherent grit by first engaging students' interests on a more personal level. Students can then expand their ideas of what is possible for them. Students must use agency to apply their own grit, but teachers can support or suppress the initial goal ideation process.

The research in this book specifically "adds" particular dimensions to the elements described as "absent" in existing grit research, mentioned at the end of Chapter 1. First, I give particular attention to social contexts, observing how the individuals I interviewed learned to navigate opportunity structures in their lives (e.g., schools, higher education, and enrichment programs) and began to exhibit help-seeking behavior. Second, I include a dynamic view of culture and interpret how students reconcile different attitudes and behaviors toward education, while fostering goals related to and conducive to achievement. Finally, I investigate the role of various support systems by identifying the role of social and cultural capital in individuals' lives.

Duckworth's perspective is generally that grit is not just inheritable through nature (one's parents and genes) but, rather, largely affected through dimensions of nurture. Essentially, grit can be taught, learned, and practiced. This idea goes against the deficit perspectives that other champions of grit have sometimes attached to the concept, assuming that some students do not have the tough mentality it takes to succeed. On the contrary, levels of grit as Duckworth envisions can be fostered in all students *if* they are provided with the right types of guidance, institutional supports, and opportunities they need to make gains.

Thinking about agency in particular is useful for insisting that we must also pay attention to the many social factors that play important roles in achievement—students' home and school environments, the mentors around them, and the opportunities they have to learn and try new things. Asking about agency and where students have room to grow also allows us to identify additional factors they may need to thrive. In the chapters that follow, I identify what those factors, resources, and opportunities can look like.

STUDYING EXCEPTIONAL CASES
TO BROADEN THE UNDERSTANDING OF DISADVANTAGE

In terms of social mobility in the United States, only around 6% of individuals born in the lowest income quintile can be expected to rise out of poverty and make it into the top income quintile in their lifetimes (Marsh, 2011). Members of high-income groups who belong to marginalized racial groups will experience less success than their White economic peers (Chetty et al., 2018). While these statistics might strengthen the structuralist camp, whose members argue that background matters the most, it is also important not to overlook the fact that a small number of individuals *are* able to transcend the socioeconomic limits of their birth and climb highly exclusive ladders. There is a story about the power of human agency within these cases.

Therefore, examining outliers or exceptional cases might help shed light on people's capabilities to navigate rigid social structures and achieve goals. I apply this premise to education by learning from students who managed to overcome significant episodic obstacles and structural barriers in their lives. The wisdom they share is in the form of stories about how they achieved academic and professional success. I listened to them and methodically found themes across individual stories to find common elements of their experiences that helped foster agency. Those findings are what fill the majority of this book.

There is an important scientific limitation that must be noted in studying the subgroup selected for my research. Learning from the subject population will not allow for sweeping generalizations about what absolutely allows others who are similarly disadvantaged to succeed. However, sharing firsthand accounts from those who successfully navigate extreme disadvantages allows for additional discovery through an inductive process. No one can or should claim to know how all people operate. The insight of qualitative research—asking people who have something in common with one another for their stories and seeking to find themes across them—is not to make generalizations about an objective truth.

Recognizing the often-overlooked, amazing feats people can achieve despite the challenges they experience should be helpful to better understand the human experience—and will ideally lead us to developing better ideas on how to help others in similar situations.

What people care about—what brings nourishment to their soul—is deeply personal. And so, I am eternally grateful to the participants for opening up to me and shedding light on their quests toward fulfillment. Presenting these stories is my way of speaking into the often-distracting scholarly landscape by sticking to the basic aims of education. I believe that fostering student agency, or the amount of influence students have over their own lives, including their ability to navigate obstacles and leverage resources, should be a basic aim within the changing trends of education.

As part of my research, I assess how young adults with disadvantages can increase their agency in the structural conditions that shape their opportunities and outcomes. These individuals operate in a space that leads to marginalization due to levels of complexity between social groups they feel both part of and alienated from. Patterson and Fosse (2015) describe this type of social disconnection:

> The reproduction of rules and resources is, of course, the unconscious learning of the procedural knowledge of middle class life. Three themes are evoked in this process: [positive] resistance and contestation, the importance of the peer group, and the structural location of the family. It is precisely in this interplay of social structure and human agency that [low-income minority] youth appear to lose their way. (p. 57)

Maybe it's not that these youth lose their way so much as we lose them on their way. But one thing is clear: Because understanding middle-class norms is important to succeeding in mainstream America, if students of color also come from disadvantaged backgrounds, they can experience a doubly hindering position.

Also, as Patterson and Fosse mention, explicitly calling attention to the dynamic relationship between structure and agency is important in understanding how students can lose or find their way on the pathways to social mobility. The duality must be considered when hypothesizing about how students can reengage as active participants in the social system and create positive change in their own lives, which is exactly what this book explores from a practical standpoint.

Unequal conditions can be internalized and make some students (rightfully) question whether schooling—and the way in which it is rigidly structured—is actually relevant and beneficial to their lives. Therefore, a major goal of my work is to learn how young people who were born and raised with limited resources can be empowered to buy into education while simultaneously drawing upon what they have learned from their environments and the people in them. The insights offered by participants in my research may help make systems more effective for students who are typically marginalized and underserved.

The exceptional cases I introduce will also reveal how tailored support systems can enable students to form academic identities. My study also tries to account for the dynamic nature of culture by addressing how culture and behavior might be influenced by outside factors such as mentors and curriculum (Chapter 6). Instead of addressing culture from a deficit perspective, the argument I make is that the only deficiency these students have had is not being afforded a comparable number of experiences and opportunities from which to learn and grow as their more privileged peers.

Accordingly, I attempt to use person-first language to respect the dignity of participants, for instance, using "students with disabilities" in place of "disabled students" (Blaska, 1993).

Learning about the achievements of students who have structural odds stacked against them, as well as locating common factors that facilitate achievement, allowed me to generate hypotheses on how success might be possible for students in similar situations. My qualitative approach is commonly used in studies that make sense of achievement, school contexts, and class status (MacLeod, 1987; Noguera, 2009; Willis, 1977). For my framing, it is valuable to view the relationship between structure and agency in a dialectic rather than in opposition, to best observe how individuals are supported or encumbered by various systems in their lives.

Some influential scholars have documented interactions between structure and agency, but with an interpretive focus on reasons for failure rather than on achievement. Their stance might seem aligned to the structuralist and overly deterministic positions that focus on indelible problems, but sometimes they also discuss broad "cultural" problems or "deficits" of the specific groups being studied (Patterson & Fosse, 2015). Such deficit perspectives are akin to alternative versions of individual responsibility theory, overlooking structural effects on culture and primarily drawing parallels between choices and behaviors to dispositions.

In education literature, culture has long received unnecessary attention and wrongful credit for determining student outcomes. Cultural deficit models postulate that underachieving students come from home cultures or socioeconomic backgrounds that are oppositional to learning (Collins, 1988; Gorski, 2011, 2016). They often have a unilateral view of what constitutes "good" or productive culture and do not always address the idea that culture is malleable and adaptable to different contexts.

John Ogbu's (1992) research, which continues to be controversial, involves the study of immigrants (who immigrated here voluntarily) and Black minorities (whose ancestors were brought here to be enslaved) to understand why the former group of students achieved more academically compared to the latter. Ogbu addresses the structural context of his students, including the socioeconomic differences that grow from opportunity gaps between immigrant families and families in the historically marginalized, perpetually disenfranchised Black American group. He also recognizes the function and reality of schools in these different settings, though schools with high populations of students who are immigrants, minorities, and Black Americans are often comparable in terms of physical resources. He thus presents findings related to a difference in culture within the school settings of these two groups.

Ogbu identified what he called an "oppositional culture" to schooling embodied or exhibited by nonimmigrant Black American students; while he found that Black students were often aware of the structural limitations in their lives, such as diminished access to work opportunities via the "job ceiling," he also took an extra step to also argue that they tended to respond by expressing disdain for the system at large.

As a result, Ogbu's research suggested that Black students often connected scholastic achievement to selling out or "acting White." He observed that immigrant students of color, who did not have a shared history of American slavery and oppression, did not exhibit the same patterns of disidentification from academics as their Black American counterparts did. While Ogbu's theory pertains to group dynamics, its ultimate focus on Black students' perceived behavior—or their apparent refusal to take advantage of educational opportunities—does not satisfactorily account for other structural forces, or for how lack of access to forms of social and cultural capital might shape the views and decisions of youth.

Still, more mainstream theories sometimes adopt Ogbu's perspectives in applications that make even more damning claims about individuals who underachieve. For instance, one theory is that low performers, particularly Black students, are prone to viewing themselves as victims by embodying a victimhood culture (McWhorter, 2000). In assessing factors that may contribute to the achievement gap, linguist John McWhorter (2000) asserted that people of color are often prone to self-sabotaging behavior rather than to a desire to take advantage of the opportunities available and presented to them. (To me and many of my colleagues, these bodies of work simply advance deficit perspectives when perhaps we should instead be focused on how asset-based approaches can reengage students by leveraging their strengths.)

Ogbu and McWhorter overlook the idea that culture is a fluid and dynamic product of environmental and temporal circumstances. For example, Angel Harris (2011) debunked McWhorter's idea by explaining that there were historically "extraordinary efforts made by Blacks to obtain an education, a trend that actually began prior to the northern benevolence and the Emancipation Proclamation" (p. 48), showing that it is narrow-minded to label an entire race as strongly adhering to any one cultural viewpoint in all circumstances.

More recently and alternatively, an example of using culture to explain achievement is the "Tiger Mother" method of parenting. Tiger Mothers are supposedly extremely demanding parents, often from Asian backgrounds, who foster in their children specific character traits, such as impulse control, that are relevant for success (Chua, 2011; Chua & Rubenfeld, 2014). The logic also implies alignment to deficit modeling, through the extension that children reared by less demanding parents fail because their parents did not instill the same values and drill the same traits into them as the more demanding parents do for their children. The idea is further limited by failing to account for the existing forms of social and cultural capital that families have and pass down to their children, nor do they fully consider the socioemotional well-being of the children being parented (Pomerantz, Ng, Cheung, & Qu, 2014).

By contrast, my book rests upon a premise that cultural dynamics cannot be considered separate from structural forces, especially given that culture and decisionmaking are influenced by and reactive to such forces (Gorski, 2016). Through examples, I will show that some parents make immense contributions to their children's academic and professional mindsets through example-setting, despite obviously challenging circumstances that arise through poverty.

The issue with deficit perspectives is primarily that they tend to view racially and/or socioeconomically marginalized students' performances in terms of perceived weaknesses rather than seeing potential in their strengths. Because I am inherently optimistic, my project instead attempts to locate and celebrate the strengths and giftedness that students might manifest through various cultural forms (skills, talents, interests), some of which may not traditionally be tied to success by mainstream views in education (Ford & Grantham, 2003; Gorski, 2011, 2016). As the old saying goes: What you pay attention to, grows.

Rather than using a structure–agency framework to explain the failure of marginalized groups, I locate instances of success and thus also realms of possibility for all students, ideally to work against deficit perspectives. I aim to uncover where students with disadvantages are full of potential, rather than deficit, and opine on how to build upon those strengths and "hidden forms of giftedness" (Gorski, 2011). My claim here is that success could be possible for any student, regardless of background or circumstance, if only collective responsibilities were raised to educate her and provide her with the right types of supports, which must be mindful of her identity, to then bolster her capacity to take on the world. Focusing on failure and deficit is too easy a trap for absolving communities from realizing that education is a social endeavor.

Because this book relates to the study of student agency in particular, I pose a larger theoretical objection to cultural- and individual-centric perspectives of achievement; theories of individualism are not adequate substitutes for the concept of human agency, which has traditionally been considered a product of the relationships among social structures, culture, and behavior (Barker, 2003; Hurrelmann, 1988; Patterson & Fosse, 2015). In other words, even in the classic disciplinary dilemma, "agency" has never stood in for simply meaning "innate ability"—because there is no such thing in our socially constructed world.

Hopefully, by now you are willing to consider that in school contexts, explaining achievement by focusing on individualism alone can underplay various "sociopolitical contexts" of education—contexts that affect how a school and class functions (Nieto & Bode, 2005, p. 7; Yosso, 2005). These cultural- and individual-focused perspectives also ignore many ideologies, or a society's "accepted ideas and values" (Nieto & Bode, 2005, p. 7). In other words, the champions of these ideas do not question why values have come to exist in the first place, nor why they have become so accepted. Ideologies are what shape culture and the opportunity structures that grow from them.

Thus, it is also important to examine how schools, which are responsible for socializing students and for perpetuating mainstream ideas, including "rugged individualism," can be complicit in the process of championing values like meritocracy at the expense of addressing marginalization. After this reflection, we can figure out how to use schools and other educational institutions to break patterns of oppression.

I have heretofore defined "agency" in a way that accounts for both the control that an individual has over a situation and the structural forces that shape a person's access and ability to leverage opportunity. At this point, it is important to establish a more robust and functional definition of agency so that it can be more identifiable in individuals who navigate all terrains of daily life.

AGENCY REDEFINED AND OPERATIONALIZED

My definition of agency grows out of this central premise: students' educational attitudes, goals, and achievements are malleable products of their experiences and social interactions, and these particular contexts, which are also shaped by cultural norms, enable students' continued development (Brofenbrenner, 2009; Neal & Neal, 2013).

The following definition draws on and synthesizes various existing versions of agency from foundational works in various fields of study: Agency is context specific. While it can manifest through action and outcome, agency can also be promoted by internalized qualities like self-efficacy or one's belief in one's ability to succeed (Bandura, 1982). Agency can be exhibited through resistance, as a means of expressing individualism (Genovese, 1976; Kelley, 1996), but more importantly, successful and productive agency benefits from critical thinking on one's social position and deliberate efforts taken to change one's circumstances for the better (Freire, 1968/1972; Kundu, 2016, 2018; MacLeod, 1987). It is related to the unique circumstances and social position of each person assessing his specific capacities for change (Giroux, 1983; Kundu, 2016, 2017).

One of the first distinctions to make regarding agency is that it is more contextual than a person simply taking an action. Anthropology, which studies human action and agency, often through ethnography, stresses the importance of being context-specific to differentiate agency from such basic action. For example, Clifford Geertz (1973) asserted that ethnography generates its importance from unlocking that microscopic, "complex specificness" or "circumstantiality" of given situations (p. 22).

However, agency, like all human action, is particular and so cannot be bound or understood predictably "as subject to stringent laws" (Boas, 1940, p. 640). By viewing agency as specific, anthropologists claim that it does not have a single form or function that is universally applicable to all scenarios. Essentially, agency gives humans greater influence over their own fates and external determinants, though different situations leave different amounts of space for exercising one's free will.

Historians have added to the idea that agency also means not simply being at the mercy of external forces. Agency can be viewed in terms of resistive action, which may be more subtle, through means of identity production, or more direct, such as collective acts of resistance. Eugene Genovese (1976), in *Roll, Jordan, Roll: The World the Slaves Made*, examined how those who were enslaved, even in the most dehumanizing conditions, retained their dignity by building their own unique culture. Slaves expressed resistance not only through escape or violent rebellion but also through music and religion, producing and taking ownership of their own individual and group identities in resistance to the system of chattel slavery.

Agency can thus also be identified in acts that work to produce an individual or collective identity. This is a characteristic that is displayed by participants in my research, elaborated upon in Chapter 5, as they negotiated the integration of their existing cultural identities with the academic and professional identities that they were developing.

In *Race Rebels,* Robin Kelley (1996) shows how agency can be located in acts of explicit resistance and rebellion. Kelley explored how Black working-class individuals and groups in post–World War II America showed agency in their acts of resistance against institutional and social racism. Their collective organizing and acts of disruption to everyday life, such as bus boycotts, were forms of civil disobedience that brought about large changes. Importantly, Kelley's work shows how agency can also be collective in nature, which is a key characteristic of my research, and is ideally useful for schools and other social institutions interested in cultivating agency to promote student success.

It is important to note that resistance cannot always overcome the structural forces of inequality nor improve a person's conditions by itself. In sociologist Paul Willis's 1977 study of the social and structural nature of disadvantage, *Learning to Labor*, the disruptive "Lads," or working-class boys, resisted dominant cultural attitudes. They acted out in class, smoked publicly, and engaged in rampant sex to go against conforming to the mainstream. The Lads saw their schooling as part of a system that oppressed working-class youth like themselves—school was a tool of social and cultural reproduction—and they resisted it by becoming oppositional to education, similar to the phenomenon described by John Ogbu (1992).

However, resistance alone is not a form of agency; resistance by itself cannot necessarily change an individual's situation or outcomes. As I define it, agency requires choice-making and deliberate action related to one's goals, similar to the way that grit does. While the Lads were rightfully suspicious of educational systems, their thoughts and actions were not calculated enough to bring about any positive changes. Willis concluded that the Lads' nonconformity (or meditated inactions) became barriers to social mobility, leading the Lads to remain in the working class. The Lads ended up where they began, locked into their original class positions. In contrast, the individuals who are highlighted in this book used agency to actively participate in the process, which improved their social and economic positions.

To be sure, some forms of resistance in school can, of course, be beneficial to cultivating an academic identity and the agency that the identity can offer. For instance, millennial students of color who identify as LGBTQ are often marginalized by their own racial groups, as well as by society (Cohen, 2010). This is particularly challenging in schools, where there is often the greatest danger to social identity formation along with stereotype threat (Hanselman, Bruch, Gamoran, & Borman, 2014; Steele & Aronson, 2005). In other words, due to the constant social grooming within school walls, adolescent students can be particularly vulnerable to how others perceive them.

However, these LGBTQ millennials are often academically successful, perhaps because of their ability to constantly navigate and reconcile their multiple identities (race, sexual orientation, or academic)—a navigation that they often perform by resisting both school and society. Holland and Cohen (2005) argue that these students' resistance promotes success in concert with critical thinking and activism; these are two more of the multiple identities that these students must embrace to be successful. In essence, this embrace—this integration of the multiple identities of the self rather than the shunning of particular identities—can itself be thought of as resistance.

The ability to look inward, the mental and perhaps more subjective component of agency—the requirement that people have confidence that they can affect their environments—appears in psychologist Albert Bandura's work on self-efficacy. Self-efficacy describes a person's reflective belief in their ability to control their own behavior to produce a specific, desired performance (Bandura, 1977, 1986, 1997). Bandura found that the "self-efficacy mechanism" was largely responsible for achievement aspirations, growth of interests, and career pursuits.

Self-efficacy channels a person's confidence in their ability to control their environment by moderating their own behaviors. Improving one's self-efficacy seems to increase one's subjective beliefs about one's agency; it does not, however, fully address how thought can manifest into behavior, or how self-efficacy beliefs translate into action (a question addressed in the following section). Agency thus also requires that a person believe, on some level, that they *can* in fact change their situation.

To carry out a desired change in any situation, one must have a belief in one's ability that is grounded and rationalized as part of fact. In other words, agency benefits from a critical assessment and reflection of the situation at hand and of one's own capabilities within that situation. The sociophilosophical work of Paulo Freire offers a helpful perspective on how to teach students this kind of critical reflection. Freire's (1968/1972) framework, which was inspired by his experiences with the Brazilian education system, argues that pedagogy is social and that teachers should increase their students' praxis (i.e., action and reflection). The primary goal of education, according to Freire, is to emancipate students from marginalized and oppressed social positions through critical thinking.

By reflecting critically on their social positions, students can increase their self-efficacy and realistically learn how to break free from their "limit situations" (Freire, 1968/1972). Students, guided by teachers, learn to see where they are subject to broader structural forces in their lives; this critical reflection enables them to choose the best action to create change in their situation. Freire's theory offers a framework for how interactions influence perceptions (a key notion in my examinations of support systems), or circuits of social and cultural capital that participants gain access to by developing procedural knowledge. Freire's work thus helps to round out my redefinition of agency.

This definition is well suited to answer my underlying research question, which I stated in Chapter 1: How do students who are initially socially and economically disadvantaged explain what it takes to overcome significant obstacles and succeed? Each of the aforementioned components of agency (context-specific action, goals linked to identity, positive resistance, and critical thinking) is necessary for recognizing the duality between structural forces and agency (the social and individual), or the possibilities for individuals to assess the challenges in their environment and their potential to overcome them. Furthermore, this definition of agency implicitly recognizes and includes structures as real and important factors in life, without simply overweighting the individual as omnipotent.

Grit as a Concept to Provide Action to Agency

More recent education research on school contexts has defined agency more subjectively, in terms of thought rather than action:

> The ability to make choices about and take an active role in one's life path, rather than solely being the product of one's circumstances. Agency requires the intentionality and forethought to derive a course of action and adjust course as needed to reflect one's identity, competencies, knowledge and skills, mindsets, and values. (Nagaoka, Farrington, Ehrlich, & Heath, 2015, p. 2)

Similarly, traditional definitions describe agency mostly in terms of subjective beliefs—including ideas of having "intentionality" and "forethought"—about one's ability (Hitlin & Kirkpatrick Johnson, 2015). In a sense, this description has made agency hard to differentiate from self-efficacy. It is clear that agency remains a highly subjective concept and thus should be aimed at forming an understanding of the actual action-oriented choices individuals make to affect their life trajectories (Kwon, 2017).

Though access to opportunity is subject to many structural forces—especially those relating to neighborhood demographics, race, and class—education does in fact still enable students from all backgrounds to better their life chances (Carter, 2003; Duncan & Murnane, 2014; Willis, 1977). An examination of how beliefs translate into action is thus integral to understanding how exceptional students, such as the participants in my research project, are able to overcome the structural forces working against them.

Sociologists Emirbayer and Mische found agency to be more of a process, embedded within social life and a part of the interaction an individual has with others (Emirbayer & Mische, 1998). In this theory, agency is temporal, informed by the past or habitual aspects, geared toward the future in relation to alternative courses, and rooted in the present from an evaluative perspective (Emirbayer & Mische, 1998). Related to the future, one aspect of agency that is fairly operationalized is the idea of "planful competence" (Clausen & Jones, 1998). Planful competence refers to an individual's ability to plan for the future and then adhere to the plan they charted (Clausen & Jones, 1998; Shanahan, Hofer, & Miech, 2003).

Grit, unlike agency, relates to how an individual moves from conceiving a goal to then enacting the process for obtaining it. Grit explicitly includes longitudinal (over time) attention for actions taken by means of goal setting and achievement (Duckworth, 2016). Grit is expressed by an individual who focuses on pursuing specific objectives over the course of an extended period of time, persisting toward goals despite challenging obstacles.

Thus, the concept of grit is useful to understand how agency relates to the purposeful action and effort taken by individuals to affect their life outcomes. For instance, one way that individuals might use grit at its highest levels is through engaging in deliberate practice over long periods of time (Duckworth, Kirby, Tsukayama, Berstein, & Ericsson, 2011). This is the idea behind the "10,000-hour rule," mentioned by Malcolm Gladwell (2008) in *Outliers*, as the practice requirement to gain mastery of a skill. Agency and grit are necessary components to every person's success, and while they are distinct, they seem to overlap in a core fashion that puts people on the path they need to reach their goals.

The Participants Who Gave This Book Voice

Before you read on, it is important for you to know at least the very basics about the people who participated in this study (for more detail about my selection process, access to, and recruitment of these folks, and for a sense of the risk factors and challenges these individuals shared, please refer to the Appendix). Without the help of these individuals, there would be no research, no findings, and no book. They seemed eager—perhaps more accurately, many mentioned that they thought it was important—to open up about how they were able to get on a path to success, with the hope that others would learn from these trials and tribulations.

To protect their identities and to give them freedom of expression, I represent the subjects with aliases, which most chose themselves, based on something or someone important to them[1]. For those who had no preference or did not want to pick an alias, I selected something (probably less creative) myself.

In return for their time and thoughtful reflection, I aim to give some voice to these individuals to participate in the ongoing, societal and/or scholarly discussions that seek to understand them and their experiences. We often try to describe, explain, or predict why some students succeed and others don't, without actually bringing these very people to join us at the table, when their perspectives might actually be the most insightful.

My goal was to create a sample pool that closely mirrored the population of youth that generally make up New York City's public school system with respect to race, income, and immigration status. According to the New York City Department of Education (2018), of the 1.1 million NYC public school students (a population akin to the size of Dallas, TX), 74% are economically disadvantaged (which was one of my qualifiers for participation), and 82% are racial minorities. By bringing together a similar subset of "high achievers," all of whom are people of color who came from economically disadvantaged backgrounds, I was able to think about their achievements and experiences within this wider context. My findings, though not generalizable to all similar students (as I have admitted), are helpful as we think about basic supports and resources that could help students who share similar backgrounds.

Because my main objective has been to learn from students who have successfully navigated around various disadvantages, let me explain how I defined "experiencing success." Generally, I categorized success the way most people functionally think about it in mainstream society. I picked participants who matched at least one of the following descriptions, which are traditionally associated with academic success and social mobility in the United States: (a) individuals currently enrolled in, registering into, or graduated from a 4-year college that grants a traditional bachelor's degree; (b) individuals who are currently enrolled in an associate's degree program and have concrete plans to attend a bachelor's-degree granting program; or (c) individuals who have graduated with at least a bachelor's degree and are currently working in a highly professionalized career track (e.g., law, medicine, government, engineering, finance) or are pursuing a graduate-level degree. More than 70% of the participants in my study attended colleges with less than a 50% acceptance rate, and 20% attended "elite colleges," schools breaking the *U.S News and World Report* college rankings top-20 list.

My sample for this research project includes 50 participants.[2] There are an equal number of male (25) and female (25) participants; 48 of them explicitly identified as coming from a racial minority background, and 44 of them were between 19 and 29 years of age at the time of the interview.[3] By studying this age range, or what many social scientists refer to as a population of "emerging adults," I was able to hear from people who are just beginning to explore their life possibilities. To an extent, this helped me think about what trends and cultural values to expect from the general population in the United States, as I learned about religious, political, and other important views young adults hold (Arnett, 2014; Arum & Roksa, 2014). At the same time, I am of course mindful that 50 participants does not make a very large sample. I will address some limitations of this in the Appendix, but I have also attempted to share with you some of the most important, broadly applicable themes that helped these students become the exceptional people they are today. I hope these findings can help other students do the same.

CHAPTER 3

The Home and Family

The elements of nurture, the where and how children grow up, might make up the most important influences that will determine their futures. A child's access to opportunities and resources depends largely on the zip code in which they are born and the characteristics of the neighborhood in which they grow up (Fruchter et al., 2012; Sharkey, 2013). The neighborhoods where my research participants were raised exhibit the lowest college readiness rates in New York City and are areas that have drastically worse school and community resources than other parts of the city (Fruchter et al., 2012; Kozol, 2012). Simply put, these blemishes greatly hurt students' chances of achieving at high levels and climbing the social ladder. A 2019 report by the organization EdBuild showed that majority-White public school districts receive, on average, $23 billion more in annual funding than non-White public school districts do, mostly because of neighborhood lines, even though they have about the same number of students.

If we imagine that all of the above make up the big picture of a somewhat grim structural reality, there has to be a smaller picture too when asking, How do children function and sometimes even thrive despite the large-scale obstacles they implicitly, maybe unknowingly, inherit and encounter routinely? The answer, first and foremost, is family. In our interviews, my participants offered their insights into the crucial and layered ways in which their family members had helped them learn to navigate their educational opportunities and environments. A major goal for family units and parent-guardians is to champion educational values while encouraging children to explore a variety of interests. This allows students to form the strong value-based foundation needed to build up their academic competencies over the years and to develop the agency needed to thrive in college and career. My participants' parents' behavior, and—for some of them—the pressures of becoming parents themselves, had great impact on the ways in which they described their journeys. This chapter delves into these themes and offers more direct quotes; I elevate their voices here to give life to the theories that grounded my research questions.

PARENTING AMID STRUCTURAL LIMITATIONS

For children of wealthy parents, the road they walk on is paved with gold. In wealthy homes, parents constantly negotiate more valuable opportunities for their children (Lareau, 2002; Lipman, 1998; Noguera, 2003; Boykin & Noguera, 2011), and in the sociology of education, Bowles and Gintis's (1976) landmark study showed that a person's projected educational attainment over their lifetime—the highest degree that they will receive—is most predicted by their parents' socioeconomic status. They found that "among children with identical IQ test scores at ages six and eight, those with rich, well-educated, high status parents could expect a much higher degree of schooling than those with less-favored origins" (Bowles & Gintis, 1976, p. 57).

Though nearly 50 years have passed since this study, the unfortunate truth of Bowles and Gintis's work is that their findings are just as true today. The Pell Institute's (2018) report on higher education equity indicators in the United States documented a 68% gap in college attainment between the highest and lowest income brackets. According to the study, in 2016, 77% of high-income students completed college; only 9% on the low-income end did. And before jumping to meritocratic explanations for this, remember how those in the top tax brackets—who are already poised for comparative success based on greater access to opportunities—can game the system. In the spring of 2019, the public was alarmed to learn that many wealthy parents and celebrities were using forms of bribery to get their children into the colleges of their choosing.

Beyond providing their children with physical resources, parents influence their kids' abilities to successfully navigate the outside world because the social and cultural environment of the home shapes the ways young people make meaning of their world. The way young people are reared plays a big role in how they are able to acquire various forms of capital in the future (Bourdieu, 1986; Lareau, 2002; Trainor, 2010).

You will recall from the Introduction that Joe Hernandez did not realize the full value of experiences, such as studying at home, until he moved to his aunt's neighborhood in New Jersey. In that Edison suburb, most of his classmates' parents had established rules requiring their children to study for extended hours to receive certain rewards. As a kid, Joe noticed this, recognized that there must be some value to these principles, and implemented them in his own life. In contrast, parents with fewer resources may experience more structural barriers to participating in their children's educational activities (Lareau, 2002; Lee & Bowen, 2006; Trainor, 2010). A parent who has to hold down two part-time, labor-intensive jobs is probably less able to check in on their kids' homework or join the Parent Teacher Association. Not only that, but parents who struggle financially also experience copious amounts of stress, which can lead to serious psychological and physiological problems for them and their children (Santiago, Wadsworth, & Stump, 2011).

In contrast, middle- and upper-class parents can more easily facilitate their children's socialization to middle-class norms through heavy involvement in their activities. According to Annette Lareau (2002), through methods of "concerted cultivation," parents with more resources often fill their children's schedules with organized activities, routinely stress the importance of asking questions in educational settings, and teach their children that they are entitled to speak with adults who have authority. This type of parenting promotes individualization by helping children realize that there are multiple opportunities for them to take advantage of in life (Lareau, 2002, 2011). Concerted cultivation is an example of providing the "procedural knowledge" that helps a child develop the ability to navigate the social and institutional settings of middle- and upper-class life while also learning to employ reasoning skills and variations of language (Patterson & Fosse, 2015).

On the other end of the spectrum, students who lack the types of specialized nurturing that facilitate entry into the middle class may feel less comfortable and less confident in academic settings; in fact, many of my participants described feeling uneasy and unsure of themselves in classroom environments, which often reward the types of dominant cultural capital that students from disadvantaged backgrounds may not so readily obtain at home (Khan, 2012; Ladson- Billings, 2006; Ransaw & Majors, 2016).

The goal of mentioning these factors is not to use them as excuses for students who struggle to "make it" out of their circumstances but rather as a reality check of the visible and invisible ways in which success can be challenging. In this chapter, I will show how, despite strong impediments, children can be taught to develop habits and attitudes that allow them to thrive academically, professionally, and socially. Though I heard many stories from students who did not grow up in supportive homes, and heard how maltreatment from parents stunted socialization to a large degree, I will focus on what parenting for success despite obstacles looks like. I will describe how particular sets of values and home-life stability can increase agency despite the limitation of financial struggles.

How Strong-Willed Parents Instill Educational Values That Foster Agency and Grit

Though all of my participants grew up in poverty, most of them credited the strong foundations of their homes as being key to their value systems and their eventual appreciation for education, an idea that is prevalent in relevant research (Ainsworth-Darnell & Downey, 1998; Harris, 2011; Kao, 2004; Mickelson, 1990). More than half ($n = 28$) of my participants recalled having strong-willed parent or guardian figures at home who shaped them in formative ways, often by stressing the importance of education and finding ways to support them and their siblings despite the structural limitations they faced on a daily basis. Many of these guardians believed that getting ahead in the United States requires a strong educational foundation and stressed this as fact to their children (Davis-Kean, 2005; Kao, 2004; Mickelson, 1990). To an extent, this simple finding contradicts the notion of oppositional culture I mentioned earlier, which suggests that some families and students are suspicious or apathetic toward education. These kinds of views are overly generalist when it comes to understanding the totality of experiences that underserved students have.

Leading by Example: Transmitting Work Ethic Through "Value Education"

"Sunny" is a Black male who grew up with a single mother in the Bronx. His mom worked multiple jobs while she finished her graduate degree so that she could provide him the most basic resources. He told me in our interview that watching his mom persevere through these challenges helped him to develop the context for putting his own goals and struggles into perspective. Sunny described his mother's work ethic to me, saying:

> It definitely made me a better person. My mom graduated from Columbia with a master's in social work, but she had a lot of obstacles to face. That showed me the attitude, "You can make anything happen if you really go after it." Some of her decisions, like having kids young, defined her being in that difficult position. She told me that, "Going to college at 22 instead of 18, don't let that set you back. Don't be self-conscious about things like that. Keep on pushing forward."

Sunny took his mom's advice, following suit by deciding that it would be best to go to college a little later in life. He took a break after high school to gain some work experience for a couple of years before enrolling in an associate's program at a local community college. Sunny's foresight in creating a plan that was best suited to meeting his immediate (financial) and future needs is a form of critical thinking that is necessary to having agency. Sunny credits his mom for instilling certain values in him that formed a strong foundation of character that he prides himself on today.

This case, and others in my work, are at odds with studies that suggest that children raised by single parents are at higher risk for delinquency (Amato & Keith, 1991; Hetherington, 2014; McLanahan & Sandefur, 1994). Instead, single parents often hold very high expectations for their children, which foster feelings of self-worth (Kundu, 2016; Slaughter-Defoe & Rubin, 2001). When parents or guardians of young people display strong will, holding work ethic as a nonnegotiable, it is perceived by and transmitted to their children over time. Furthermore, many of my participants shared the notion that they received a "value education" at home; their sense of what to prioritize in life was developed through seeing the actions and hearing the advice of guardian figures, often regarding educational pursuits (Valencia, 2002).

"Gouvia" had some of the highest praise for the power of education. She told me that even as a young teen, her lifelong goal had been to work in the field of education, so she could help other young people access educational opportunities. After college, she worked at a company that implemented technology-based advising systems to help students transfer from community college to 4-year colleges. After 2 years in that position, she transitioned into working at the New York City Department of Education. Gouvia's accomplishments are extraordinary and uplifting, given her story. Her mother passed away when she was just 14 years old, shortly after her family had moved to the United States. When I asked Gouvia what makes her unique, she gave me an answer that almost sounds like a brochure for the power of having grit:

> [What makes me unique is] my motivation when it comes to education. I'm very dedicated to finishing my work and I've always been a great student. I value my education over my social life, for instance. If I had to choose, I definitely value academics more. Also, I'm always thinking about the future—how to set myself up for success. I'm very goal-oriented and always have that end goal in mind, for sure.

The very definition of grit, Gouvia exhibits a "passion and perseverance for [her] long-term goals" (Duckworth, 2016), as demonstrated not only by her commitment to her own education but also by her dedication to a professional life that will help educate others. She has maintained a single-minded focus on her goal because she believes in the transformational power of education, and she is driven by her values, which motivate her desire to spread educational equity.

I asked her if there were certain factors in her upbringing that influenced her decision to make a difference in her community through education. She explicitly connected her own work ethic, strong character, and appreciation for academics to her mother:

> I grew up in Jamaica in a very small, rural community. The only way to really get out of that community was through education. My mom was very supportive, in order for me to do well—she always came out for parent–teacher conferences to make sure I was on track academically. She didn't have a chance to get the best education that she wanted. She graduated from high school but never continued after

that, so she wanted to make sure her children got much further than she did in life. Especially because she had a sister who went all the way through school and ended up being very successful. She wanted that for her kids.

With her mother's guidance and values, Gouvia developed agency and critical thinking from a young age, which included the ability to compare her mother's and her aunt's lives and to better visualize the effects of certain goals in her own future. The impact Gouvia's mother had on her life was so strong that even after her mom passed, Gouvia persisted and became her own educational advocate in order to realize her mother's vision as she adapted and grew up in different contexts.

These guardians' displays of hard work greatly influenced their children. The grit that Gouvia's and Sunny's mothers both displayed was directly transferred to their kids. In terms of higher education, for instance, most of my participants (above 85%) are first-generation college students, hopeful that they will be able to provide the same value education, reciprocal stability, and support to their own families. Through their parents, Gouvia and Sunny gained the perspective that a combination of hard work and a solid education would help them in life.

Raising Citizens by Stressing Education and Service

Traditionally in sociology, schools are seen as institutions where students develop a collective identity (maybe through acts of patriotism and the Pledge of Allegiance) and learn the common cultures of their community (Dill, 2007; Durkheim, 1938). In school, students also learn about their roles as contributing members of society and what is expected of them (Arum, 2005; Carnoy & Levin, 1985; Durkheim, 1938). I find that the home-sphere can also be responsible for cultivating this same type of agency (navigating the many ins and outs of participating in civic life) by passing down parents' and guardians' ideals about what it means to be a worthy American. The concept is corroborated in studies of immigrant parents of undocumented children, as well as parents in general (Hulbert, 2011; Yoshikawa, 2011): Guardians can help their children to better see their potential to make a difference in their community, rather than simply bemoaning their community's conditions.

In many cases, the parent figures I learned about used their working-class status as motivation for their kids to do better, achieve more, and break the cycle of poverty in their families; they often did so by holding their children accountable to high standards of excellence and civic duty. As I mentioned in Chapter 1, Imperial, a recent college grad, epitomizes this idea of legacy and virtue. Without his father in the picture, he was raised by the women in his family. While he describes his mother and aunts as beyond influential, his grandmother was the family matriarch and inspired him to set goals for himself. He said:

> My grandmother came from Honduras in the late sixties. She raised me. She was always brave, and she was always telling me to be innovative and to push myself educationally, and to serve the family and community in ways that other people hadn't.

One way she transmitted these values was to set strict guidelines in their shared household, and rather than chafe at the discipline, Imperial holds her in the highest regard for her hands-on approach that led him to develop lifelong ideals. His grandmother's insistence that Imperial was responsible to his family *and* his community led him to form a deep obligation toward serving the Bronx, where he grew up. He told me that he feels a strong sense of duty, as a Black male, to set a good example in his community. Other experiences, such as attending one of the few all-Black high schools in New York City, helped Imperial continue to develop racial pride, aligned to his desire to succeed. As I will discuss in the following chapter, learning about iconic Black figures in school helped Imperial want to be as successful and influential as these people.

Another way in which Imperial set goals regarding his community responsibilities was to become involved in neighborhood development in the Bronx in a way that put the community first. His grandmother fostered his agency by helping him to first understand the importance of his social position as a Bronx stakeholder through a sense of belonging, and today Imperial is about to complete a Fulbright program in Europe, where he is studying urban planning as a master's in public administration degree candidate. He hopes to contribute to the rapid influx of development in the Bronx, from a community-first perspective in which the residents are not exploited by gentrification. The notion of serving one's community appears frequently in my research, and in Chapter 5 I will elaborate on this idea as a key trait of agency.

Many other parents of my participants acted in ways that strengthened the democratic functioning of schools by giving their children a strong moral foundation. This is an especially important consideration when we apply this idea to lower-income families, who are often viewed as being culturally misaligned with mainstream society or thought of as being heavily reliant upon schools to assimilate their children (Ballenger, 1999; Bartlett & Garcia, 2011; Patterson & Fosse, 2015). On the contrary, my research shows that low-income, stable families are integral in motivating successful students who later go on to become important contributing members of society. These findings contradict recently repolarized nationalistic ideals, spearheaded by public figures such as President Donald Trump. These camps often view low-income and immigrant households as taking advantage of and exhausting available resources without making equally important contributions to society.

It seems that community-oriented values and hard work are best conveyed to children through the actions that parents take and the examples they set. Such was the case for "Edwin," a Latinx male of El Salvadoran background who was also raised by a single mother with help from his sister. Edwin's mother and sister made tremendous personal sacrifices and worked tirelessly so that he could attend a respected prep school, hoping that his education would help him get into college. They not only verbally reinforced the importance of education in climbing the American social ladder; his mother and sister also showed him through their actions. Edwin told me:

> I got into Loyola, but the scholarships they offered me were all contingent on being a citizen. I took it a little harder because for high school, my mother had put me into a private school. That was her biggest sacrifice. She said, "My biggest gift to you is this school because I can't really afford it." She worked at a travel agency, but that started to go down. She did odd jobs. She worked in laundry for a while. My sister was working too. She worked in the city in a hotel. Both of them helped to pay for this high school I went to in Jersey. Going to this all-boys school is what helped me to keep up academically for when I went to college later.

Unfortunately, Edwin was undocumented, and neither he, his mom, nor his sister realized the strict regulations that stand in the way of going to college for undocumented students (Gonzales, 2016). In spite of his hard work, Edwin was not able to go straight to college after graduating from high school, but he did go to a community college for his associate's degree after gaining work experience. This opened a pathway for him to enroll at one of the nation's consistently top-five ranked colleges (where citizenship is treated in a need-blind manner) to receive his bachelor's degree at the age of 27. He told me that in spite of a nearly decade-long gap in his education, he hadn't fallen behind because of the strong academic foundation he had received from attending the prep school.

Through their hard work, often at labor-intensive jobs, Edwin's mom and sister displayed grit, a fact that was not lost on Edwin, who recently graduated. Their goals revolved around Edwin's future, and they displayed a type of "surrogate grit," an idea researched by Dr. Angela Duckworth's Character Lab, with the premise that mentors and adults in students' lives can help teach students to be gritty toward goals through displaying grit themselves. We see this concept play out in Edwin's life as he recognized and internalized his family's efforts and later replicated similar actions in his own pursuits.

The Lasting Benefits of Stability and Structure in Childhood

Many other participants described the incredible lengths their families went to in order to offer them forms of stability, despite financial struggles, and I heard a number of stories about parents who took measures to hide the effects of poverty from their kids. This is significant because if parents and mentors can present a sense of structure in children's lives, young people can more easily form positive academic identities (Ransaw & Majors, 2016; Slaughter-Defoe & Rubin, 2001; Wyman, 1993). Not only that, but children are able to experience childhood more fully.[1] This allows them to explore various interests with more ease as well as grow up without lingering stress and its associated, negative impacts.

"Sari," a Latinx female, was raised by a single mother in the South Bronx. She told me that her mom assumed the majority of burdens in the family and, in so doing, shielded her children from feeling the constraints of having fewer resources. Though encumbered by financial stress, Sari's mom took deliberate action so that Sari actually felt financially stable. Furthermore, she did not inundate her daughter with the realities and financial complexities of living paycheck to paycheck because she was afraid it might strain Sari's childhood. Sari elaborated:

> I've really grown to respect my mom. You don't realize certain things until you're older. We would walk to A&P to get groceries and have to walk back with the bags. Later I realized, "Wow, my mom never made it a big deal that we didn't have the car, which was in the shop for weeks longer than usual until she could pay for it." She never put those stresses on me. She made some of the things that were hard seem normal. And she approached hardships with grace. I try and approach things that way now, the way she approached every difficulty with grace.

The way Sari describes her mom as having "grace" in the face of challenges could also be considered a form of grit—it reminded me again of Barack Obama's use of "grace and grit" to describe his wife, Michelle. The ability to navigate hardships with poise is an awe-inspiring trait. Today, Sari shows grace and grit in many of her responsibilities, which include commuting for 90 minutes to and from school, juggling multiple extracurricular activities, and working a part-time job at her college library.

There's a stark contrast between having to provide stability in the ways Sari's mom did—by not letting her daughter realize their car was in the shop, for example—and the ways in which middle- and upper-class parents often create stability and structure for their children through leveraging financial resources. Beyond paying for partial or full college tuition, these parents may send their children allowances during college or pay for their cellphone service. For wealthier families, these practices often continue after college, with parents welcoming their children to live rent-free at home, sometimes for years, while their children take advantage of valuable experiences such as unpaid internships and strive for financial independence (Arnett, 2001, 2014; Arum & Roksa, 2014).

Of course, young people who come from more financially supportive homes are deserving of help. All people are. It's just important to understand that these comforts provide immensely useful leg-ups for young adults who are setting the stage for their future livelihood, working to make it or to stay in the middle class. Simply put, students who have supports are at a significant advantage over those who do not. As a result, parents with lower means, like those of my participants, sometimes have to work even harder to offer their children the stability and structure critical for nurturing a similar level of success (Ransaw & Majors, 2016; Slaughter-Defoe & Rubin, 2001).

"Malcolm" is a new father whom I met in Jamaica, Queens, and as we conducted our interview on a park bench, he held his daughter. It was more than a little ironic when I learned in our first exchange that for his whole life Malcolm had had a turbulent relationship with his own mother. Malcolm described her as being "bipolar and manipulative" (he stated that she was clinically diagnosed) and said she had not offered him much warmth or support during his childhood. They fought constantly. His father was not in the picture when he was a kid, and Malcolm said he later realized that his mother's mental condition had exacerbated the factors that led to their separation. When she eventually learned that Malcolm, who was by then a teenager, was trying to reconnect with his estranged father, she kicked him out.

Malcolm then became homeless for years at a time during his young adult life; he worked the night shift as a doorman in different buildings in Manhattan and slept outside during the day. He took "bird baths" in public restrooms to stay relatively clean for work.

What really started to turn Malcolm's life around was his new girlfriend's mother, who had opened up her apartment to them after her daughter gave birth to Malcolm's child. Along with giving the young family stability and shelter, she offered what mattered the most to Malcolm—an emotional lifeline, which was something he had been desperately, and perhaps unknowingly, searching for. He finally felt that he could let down some of the trauma and heavy burdens he had carried for so long. He said:

> Ever since Maryanne was pregnant, her mom has been the biggest support. We're going to stay with her mother to save enough as possible. A lot of people say, "If you need me call," but I don't think they mean it. They say it because it sounds good. Her mother is amazing. I'd die for her, easily. I grew up struggling, so to now have

someone always there who has your back—it's unbelievable. It's weird. In my house, there were five people. We could walk down our hall and not acknowledge each other. Constant fights. When you're poor and hungry, if food isn't yours, but in the fridge, someone is going to take it. It's *Survivor*. From going from that, to being homeless, to now finding someone who gives a damn about me is like . . . wow.

Beyond the emotional and financial support she had offered to Malcolm and Maryanne, she also helped to provide the young couple with initial child support, consistent with the trend of grandparents acting as caregivers for young grandchildren (Kropf & Kolomer, 2004; Waldrop & Weber, 2001). This support system boosted Malcolm's conviction that one day he would be able to support Maryanne and their newborn on his own. The power in his words gave me no doubt that he would put his life on the line for Maryanne's mother if he needed to.

During another interview I conducted, "Hector" told me he was enrolled in a dual master's and master's in social work (MA/MSW) degree program in child development at an elite university. He also worked a full-*and* part-time job and was recently married. Given how expensive New York City is, Hector and his wife had been unable to save much money despite each of them holding down stable jobs, and they were not sure where to turn for help. Hector's parents opened their doors to the newlyweds despite having limited space because they knew, as most middle-class parents do, that a lack of savings now would be a roadblock to the young couple's future plans.

Hector told me that he had not expected to be as candid about his parents' help in our interview as he had been. Additionally, their support meant that he could afford to leave his full-time job and focus on his other responsibilities. He confided:

I feel like I'm still in this limbo area. I've done my undergrad, but my undergrad alone isn't going to take me where I want to go. Now I'm neck deep in this dual-degree graduate program, and at the same time I feel uncertainties. I'm always thinking that I need a secure job really soon. I work part-time, but if my wife wasn't working full-time, I wouldn't have the freedom to explore more education. She's a huge support. So is family. Recently—this is probably a bit more private, but it's part of my reality—we got married in July. We were living on our own for a while with no savings. My parents said, "Look, you got two more years left in this program, and it's not really a good idea to start off without savings." They opened their home to us. We moved into my parents' house in February. It's fantastic. The fact that we have that network, I feel very fortunate.

Hector mentioned that prior to receiving help in the form of housing, he felt a self-imposed pressure to forego his graduate degree and instead take a full-time job. It was his family and wife who convinced him not to, by supporting him so that he was able to focus on his studies and successfully graduate. Since our interview, I followed up with Hector and found out that he has been happily working as a bilingual family therapist at a guidance center. He and his wife also had their first child, and Hector's parents could not be more excited to be grandparents.

As Hector mentioned, the reality today is that a college degree does not necessarily carry enough weight for a person to be guaranteed entry into the middle class (Abel & Deitz, 2014; Rosenbaum & Person, 2003). Also notable is Hector's use of the word "network," which highlights the impact that someone's family structure has in furthering their academic path as an adult. Many economically disadvantaged students are forced to drop out of K–12 to try to enter the workforce early because of financial constraints (Fine, 1991; Rumberger, 2011); however, even that proves tough without an educational footing. In 2018 in New York City, it was reported that approximately 136,000 young people, aged 16 to 24, were neither working nor in school (Treschan & Lew, 2018). Nationwide, one in seven youth are "disconnected" in this way. Economic capital is still largely foundational to students' ability to acquire other forms of social and cultural capital, and parental support is a key supplement to cultural and financial capital to help set students up for life.

"GROWING UP TOO SOON": IMMENSE RESPONSIBILITIES AND NUANCED EFFECTS ON AGENCY

My participants with parents who weren't able to nurture their growth by providing structure or easing housing or other financial burdens expressed another, more nuanced, way that family structure affected them: These participants often had to take on various "adult" responsibilities as children, and as a result, they "grew up too soon." Six of my participants explicitly used language similar to "growing up too soon" while describing their upbringings to me. I heard variations such as, "I didn't have a childhood" ("Alicia") or "I was doing things that normal kids don't" ("Xavier"). Participants also revealed hard truths like, "I had to miss two, three weeks of school to watch my sister whenever my sister got sick" ("Joe"). In this section, I will briefly focus on how the particular internal feeling of having one's childhood stolen or taken away affects individual agency in multidimensional (not unilaterally good or bad) ways.

To an extent, having increased responsibility during adolescence can increase a person's *overt* agency because, on the most basic level, they simply have more mature things expected of them from early in their life. For instance, helping to take care of one's younger siblings or helping a parent read tax documents are experiences that confer significant procedural knowledge to young people. However, by the same token, it is important to acknowledge that these same responsibilities also carry heavy tolls, which can be difficult for children to manage on their own.

Recall that Gouvia, the young woman who came from rural Jamaica to the United States as a child, mentioned that her mother had *always* been her education champion and that her mother passed away when Gouvia was only 14 years old and in 8th grade. I delicately asked her how her mother's passing had affected her mentality toward education, something Gouvia had said she cared deeply for, especially due to her mother's influence. She replied:

> I started becoming my own advocate. I wanted to make *her* proud. I always reflected back on all the motivation she gave me. I knew I had to have that internal drive moving forward. In all honesty, my dad, though he definitely cared about our education, was too busy to come to school for the PTA meetings. He never made it to a parent–teacher conference; he never made it to report card night. Even though I was a star student and graduated as valedictorian of my high school. My aunt would come.

Though Gouvia's aunt filled some of the void of her mother and father's absence, Gouvia eventually stopped relying on her. She continued:

> [My aunt] came for most of my award ceremonies, parent–teacher conferences, and open-school nights. But I believe that my freshman year, one day she turned to me and said, "You know, your dad could come too sometimes." That's when I started to feel like, "She's too involved. She has her own children." I just stopped asking her from there on. I knew I didn't really have anyone focusing on me anymore (laughs).

During Gouvia's teenage years, her agency increased through her critical thinking, as well as through action toward and reflection (praxis) on her specific obstacles. She did this through self-efficacy and believing in herself. Even though Gouvia was independent and capable, once her aunt stopped regularly attending her academic events, Gouvia lacked the kind of important support that could have lightened the constant and heavy load that rested on her shoulders and her shoulders alone. She quickly, and unfortunately in some sense, came to realize that she could not rely on others to become successful. Many young people who grew up disadvantaged face situations similar to this. As I will elaborate on in Chapter 5, sometimes this leads students and other young people to develop extreme cases of burnout that are detrimental to their goals and also to their health. Gouvia remained positive and upbeat throughout our serious interview, which is a testament to her personality, to be sure, but afterward I wondered if she had been careful not to invoke self-pity or to try to generate any sympathy from me. I can still hear her laugh at the end of her statement when she spoke of her aunt mentioning her father's lack of support, which felt to me like a symbolic representation of the shield she has sometimes had to use to guard her deeper emotions.

"Alicia," age 21, similarly mentioned learning to advocate for herself and her mother from the time she was a kid. At the time of our interview, Alicia was a college senior studying education at a top private college. At multiple points in our conversation, she described experiencing a lost, stolen, or missing childhood. Early on, I had asked her to describe herself, and she replied that she was "very responsible." I probed further, to which she replied:

> I've always been a mini-adult my whole life. If there were repairs needed at my house, I called repair companies and met them at the door. As a 6-year-old. It actually doesn't matter what my age is. I have responsibilities that I can't use excuses for. I feel like most of my life I didn't have the opportunity to have a childhood like other people. I had to work really hard just to achieve my goal of getting to college. Once I got to college, *that* was kind of my childhood because we have no responsibilities aside from going to school. That was never the case for me, and it still will never be the case. I have to be an adult, do adult things, like work and take care of my little sister, and help my mom out. That's okay.

Alicia refers to the inherent privilege of others by referring to *college* as her "childhood." Perhaps she did this unknowingly, but I highly doubt it because she seemed wise beyond her years when we spoke. Alicia had worked hard throughout her childhood and teenage years to make it to an elite college. In addition to academic demands, she juggled household responsibilities and held down a part-time job. Alicia's mother was an immigrant struggling to learn English, so Alicia helped with many daily tasks such as paying bills. Navigating these different roles with "grit and grace," Alicia developed a keen ability to methodically plan for the future and prioritize her responsibilities. As a result of her circumstances, she developed more agency as she became more fully aware of her own social status in life and strategized about how to help her family break out of intergenerational poverty.

Even though she was attending one of the most academically demanding colleges in the United States, Alicia described her overall experience as relaxed and fun. As an undergraduate, she was finally able to focus on herself. She told me that her classmates did not understand how fortunate they were to have had more sheltered and comfortable childhoods. Like Gouvia and many of my other participants, Alicia knows that throughout her life she will continue to have many more responsibilities than her peers. And yet, she seems unlikely to feel blindsided by the routine challenges of adult life, like working a 9-hour workday or paying taxes. For these reasons, experiencing significant levels of responsibility from a young age is not always negative because it generally increases the agency of young people by helping them develop foresight and strategies for achieving future goals. The challenge is to capture the benefit of learning from these responsibilities without becoming overwhelmed by the stress that frequently accompanies them.

One way to support students who strive to succeed despite experiencing multiple challenges is with access to services that promote positive mental health and well-being. Without such resources, latent consequences can creep up and eventually inhibit an individual's agency and grit significantly. When young students overwork themselves the way Gouvia or Alicia have done at times, there can be harmful physical and mental effects. Sometimes these stressors build up to serious psychological ailments later in adulthood. Again, I will mention these realities in the section on student burnout in Chapter 5. These are avenues I am excited to follow for future research, as we must consider that student achievement and success should also be measured by a person's mental health and overall well-being.

YOUNG PARENTS: AN AMPLIFYING EFFECT ON AGENCY AND GRIT

Much of the research on early parenthood depicts students from low-income communities who become parents as lacking consequential thinking (Aslam et al., 2017; Langley et al., 2015), but these works focus more heavily on understanding behaviors without paying much attention to the structural conditions that may lead to certain outcomes. Typically, teenage pregnancy is connected with other youth risk factors that indicate higher probability for poor academic, health, and life outcomes (Dworsky & Courtney, 2010). Social science research shows that there is an increased likelihood for unplanned and early pregnancies in low-income communities (Henshaw, 1998; Kaye, Suellentrop, & Sloup, 2009; Lifflander, Gaydos, & Hogue, 2007), and some of my participants took on increased responsibilities through early parenthood. Although this is a fairly tricky and sometimes controversial topic, I choose to address it directly so that we can work to change the existing streams of thought that view young parents as delinquents.

A 1987 study found that approximately two-thirds of school administrators in the United States prioritized teenage pregnancy as a top-10 problem in their schools (Kenney, 1987). The Congressional Research Service reports that about 614,000 teenagers in the United States became pregnant in 2010, accounting for about 6% of all births that year (Solomon-Fears, 2016). These statistics cannot be fully understood separately from the relationship between impoverished communities and the systems of education they have access to. It is not a random fact that out of the total 14,000 districts in the United States, only 25 large urban school districts account for approximately 10% of all teen pregnancies and 20% of all high school dropouts (Shuger, 2012).

Much of the scholarship that attempts to discuss prevention uses economic analyses, perhaps estimating the social cost of high school dropouts and teenage parents. "Cost-benefit" perspectives represent a large amount of research on the topic of teenage pregnancy and young parenthood but ultimately ignore a lot of the human elements of this subject. More galling is that "young families" are often written about with hopeless and undignified language. Students are portrayed as casualties of poverty and failed educational outcomes for policymakers to ameliorate rather than individuals who could have promising futures with adequate support. But as Tupac reminds us in "Mama's Just a Little Girl," sometimes these parents are close to being children themselves. They may be as much in need of stability, nurturing, love, and care as their children are.

As I have said, one of the main goals of this book is to combat deficit perspectives applied to students who are born with less opportunity. Given the reality of teenage parenthood, alongside "prevention" research, it is important to focus on factors that might improve the educational experiences of these students (Feldman Farb & Margolis, 2016; Fernandes-Alcantara, 2018) and to specifically challenge existing deficit notions of young students who become parents. Though early pregnancy has largely been clearly linked to intergenerational inequality (Barcelos & Gubrium, 2014; Huang, Costeines, Kaufman, & Ayala, 2014), some of my participants provide examples that suggest that having a child during young adulthood, even if unexpected, can catalyze academic and professional goal formation.

Ten of my participants (seven male, three female) became parents in their teenage years. Their stories give me hope. In their own way, each of these cases shows that having a child early in one's life does not necessarily preclude long-term academic progress. I find that when resources are available, being a parent can actually increase individual agency and grit. In fact, all but one of these "parent-participants" remain highly involved in the lives of their children, using their parenthood as a motivator to keep excelling. "Roxanne" became a mom when she was 17. Her unplanned pregnancy disrupted her straightforward path to college as she took time off after high school to work and live at home. She ended up going to college after a couple years, starting with an associate's degree at a community college and then finishing her bachelor's in her mid-20s. Like many other participants, she told me that the main reason she works hard is so her child won't have the same worries that she did growing up. I probed to find out what kind of opportunities she wants for her daughter that she did not have herself:

> Well, for one, I wasn't as close to my mom as I wanted to be. She's a great person and provider, but she wasn't as nurturing as I would have liked. I didn't feel like she was open with me, which probably led to me getting pregnant earlier. If [she] was more disciplinary, and I knew I [wasn't allowed] to do certain things, it would have helped. But I did get pregnant at a young age. When I think about raising my daughter, I try to be more open, not be afraid of having conversations.

Today Roxanne is an office manager at a nonprofit organization that helps underserved youth, and she has aspirations to go to graduate school after saving up more money. Her interview reinforces the idea that having structure, stability, and even discipline in one's home is incredibly formative and beneficial for children, and her belief that if her mother had adopted a warm, yet demanding approach (Delpit, 2012), she might not have gotten pregnant at such a young age is telling. Though Roxanne is very happy to be a mom, she is aware of the additional stressors that having an unexpected pregnancy brings to a teenager. These are the kinds of constraints she wants her own daughter to be free from experiencing, ideally by learning from her example.

"Stan," a young father I interviewed, was a senior operations analyst at a tech security company when we spoke. He builds on what Roxanne says, mentioning how impressionable his toddler and other children are, which further motivates him to set strong examples for them. Stan told me:

> My relationship with my daughter has opened me up to the idea of watching the backs of young people and educating them. Seeing my daughter grow up, I've noticed that kids are so impressionable and innocent. And if innocence is crushed, there's no getting it back. When you see kids and your kid grow up, you have a willingness to do more. I feel empowered to see my daughter always learning and doing new things. She's very energetic and adventurous. Young people empower me when they see things differently, as opposed to maybe a 40-year-old who isn't happy and thinks the world is miserable.

Stan is referring to the often discontented, middle-aged people he manages. His goal is to help his daughter develop in a way that will prevent her from becoming so jaded or apathetic later in life. After all, she has shown him that the world is *not* miserable. Stan reminds me of Alicia and other participants who lamented growing up too soon, those who mentioned innocence and the fragility of childhood, and those who sometimes experienced more than they bargained for while growing up. Having a child greatly increased Stan's agency and desire to be positively influential in the lives of others. After Stan's daughter was born, he graduated from college and left what he called "a dead-end job." He confided that his daughter was a primary influence in his recent decision to switch careers and go into teaching to leave a lasting impact and legacy on other kids.

As we discussed, valuing education is a principle that individuals often receive from their guardians at home; therefore, it is not surprising to me that my parent-participants mentioned their efforts as parents to stress the importance of education to their own children. "JLo," the oldest participant in this project, is a father who finished his bachelor's degree at 44 years old. He is also someone who personifies the phrase "larger than life." I was immediately aware of his friendly nature as soon as I met him, and we sat down for our interview in the busy student lounge of his campus. During our conversation, at least four different students came over to say hi to him. Of course, they all seemed to be 20 years younger than him, but that did not affect their friendliness. JLo told me that he works extremely hard to instill educational values in his children:

> My son told me that high school kills his creativity. He hears what my daughter and I tell him about how college is so much different than high school—I just want him to get to that point. I told him that I would support him in anything he does so long as it's positive. I learned from my father—who wasn't necessarily the best father—to do the complete opposite from what he did. It worked out pretty well for me. I want them to find themselves. I'm not rushing them out of the house. I want them to be comfortable when they leave. I told my daughter: If you're pursuing your doctorate at 40, you can stay with us at home if you want to.

Through JLo's own actions and educational pursuits, he modeled the kind of grit and agency he hoped to instill in his children. As a young father, it had made the most financial sense to him to stop pursuing his education beyond a GED, but after working in chauffeuring services for more than 20 years, when JLo's teenage son told him that he aspired to be "just like him," JLo decided to go back to school to set a better example. Most of his classmates were much younger and more accustomed to traditional school settings, but after enrolling in community college, he successfully obtained his associate's and then, through tremendous grit, continued to get his bachelor's degree in his 40s from an elite college. JLo supports my finding that parents foster their children's agency by providing strong, structured support. And as a parent himself, he understands the importance of long-term financial and emotional support in the same way that

Maryanne's mother does because he mentions that he will gladly keep his home open for his kids if they need it as they transition into adulthood.

I frequently noticed that the parent-participants in my sample tended to have a heightened sense of purpose in their lives. This is corroborated by new research on young adult "turning points"—moments that can catalyze positive change for individuals' trajectories. For example, one study found that new parenthood was associated with reductions in gang membership and criminal offenses (Pyrooz, McGloin, & Decker, 2017). Just as Stan describes how his daughter helped him to realize his passion for teaching and mentoring, some of my other participants credited their children with helping them develop clarity around their ambitions.

"Esquire" is another brilliant example of this. Esquire, a moniker I gave him after hearing about his passion to use his law degree for social good, had a son when he was 20 years old. He ended up losing custody in court proceedings that followed a separation from his son's mother. He told me how much this experience impacted him and his thoughts around his future goals:

> The reason why I came to [this elite college], the reason why I continued my education, the reason why I want to study law after this, is because of a bias in the system of law. I feel there is extreme bias in family court systems. I should have custody of my son right now. I got absolutely worked over by this sleazebag and by the courts. I got told by the courts it's solely because I was doing too much, that I had a job while I was enrolled in college. Apparently [the mother's] situation, which was basically hanging out at a friend's house all day, was better to raise a child than mine.

Esquire has very recently graduated from law school, taking a step in the direction of pursuing his unwavering goal to become an attorney who serves fellow parents in court. Specifically, he has accepted a position as a defense attorney at a large defender services organization in New York City, where he will help parents from low-income neighborhoods to keep or regain custody of their children.

He was accepted into law school on a full-ride scholarship. Though it was difficult, the experience of initially losing primary custody of his son was the driving force behind the necessary grit and agency to follow this difficult path. He has a great relationship with his 10-year-old son, whom he sees regularly through what has become a joint-custody agreement with the mother. He told me that making his son proud is a huge motivator and that he is determined to set the example for his son that education is critical to advancing in life. Had it not been for the birth of his son, Esquire says, he might still be aimless—bogged down by the immense difficulties of his childhood (being kicked out of his home and experiencing periods of home-lessness and violence). I will elaborate on the idea of "purpose" in Chapter 5, addressing how it is relevant to agency, grit, and life goals.

It is important to mention that of my 10 parent-participants, only JLo and Hector remain in long-term relationships with the biological coparents of their children; both described being in happy and supportive marriages with their partners. Still, with the exception of "Xavier," who says his time in prison strained his relationship with the mother of his daughter, the other seven participants each described maintaining cordial working relationships with their biological coparents. Even Esquire, who harbors some anger to-ward the initial court decision, maintains a healthy relationship with his son's mother. Roxanne, the mother who uses the kind of warm yet demand-ing approach with her own daughter that she wishes her own mother had used with her, put this cordiality into perspective:

> I didn't grow up with my dad. It wasn't really tough on me because my mom did a really good job of raising my sisters and I. She did a good job of balancing work and providing for us. But, I definitely think about my daughter and her father's relationship. I want him to be around, which is what's happening. I didn't have that. Not that it hindered me, but it could have. I don't know how my life would have been different had he been there.

This quote is particularly revealing, especially because Roxanne men-tioned during our interview that she wished her mother had been more nurturing. From her own experience, she has learned that sometimes the greater good is maintaining a positive relationship with an ex for the benefit of the child. These efforts are what will help Roxanne's daughter to have a more stable life than she did, and remembering this is one way Roxanne deals with her own challenging childhood. Thus, these types of single-parent households can truly provide supportive environments for children, shield-ing from potential stresses and turbulence. My parent-participants all ex-hibited reflection followed by rational action, which is an example of how critical thinking contributes to agency.

CONCLUSION

The stories contained in my research challenge existing notions that low-in-come families value education less than others do, or that they can be sus-picious or even resentful of opportunity systems. In fact, even though the individuals I met mostly attended poor-performing schools, their home en-vironments remained places in which education was highly valued. Hector, the newlywed pursuing a dual master's degree and living with his parents, told me a story about the day he decided to drop out of high school and how it affected his mother:

> One of my last experiences in high school was the day I took my mother to sign me out. She wanted to speak to a counselor to see if we could think of other options. The counselor told my mother, right in front of me, "We can't change his mind. He's telling you he's going to get a GED, so just take him to a GED school." That proved that these people don't give a shit about me here. This guy proved it to me. It's so easy for him, one less to worry about. That experience convinced me that education was a lost cause. My mom was in tears. I think about how she must have felt. At that moment, I was cold to how she felt because I felt like she didn't understand. I was an arrogant teen. Now I think of this immigrant woman, who sacrificed so much of her life, and her kid, who didn't want to take advantage of everything she's worked so hard to offer him.

Even though Hector's school had failed him, his mother persisted in her hope that he would continue toward college. I find that in these types of nurturing homes, parents and children often remain in mutually giving and supportive relationships and, in the long run, are able to create a better future for the entire family. As I mentioned, when Hector decided to return to school, he relied on his parents' support, moving himself and his wife back in with them. Today, Hector remains focused on his goal to help his parents live a comfortable life once he is more established. JLo, who tells his adult kids they are welcome to use him for support as long as they are improving their futures, is similar to Hector's parents in this way.

My participants who became young parents, mostly as a result of unplanned pregnancies, work very hard to be nurturing parents. Parenthood, to an extent, was a turning point that increased their agency because they were compelled to better plan and strategize for themselves and their dependents. Even those who are separated from their children's biological coparents can still be incredibly successful at parenting, and the majority of my participants maintain positive relationships for the benefit of their children.

I learned from my participants that beyond their day-to-day lives, having a child can help them put their childhood experiences into perspective. The challenges they faced in their own upbringing helped them learn about positive and negative parenting techniques. The narratives of young family success I touched on go against many socially prevalent ideas, which include the idea that men of color are more prone to becoming absentee fathers (Neale & Clayton, 2014; Patterson & Fosse, 2015; Robbers, 2009; Sipsma, Biello, Cole-Lewis, & Kershaw, 2010). Ideally, a takeaway from my research is that if students of color, especially those who face financial and familial duress, are provided with tailored social and cultural supports, their agency toward social mobility can be fostered even if they are young parents (Kundu, 2018).

For most of my participants who missed out on the experiences of a traditional, pleasant childhood, the challenges of learning to navigate obstacles like taking care of multiple siblings while also going to school helped them develop agency. This kind of increased agency—which is often the result of overburdening oneself—can come at high costs, however, which sometimes manifest later in life. I will elaborate upon this idea in Chapter 5, which is about "The Ever-Evolving Human."

My participants had various experiences during childhood that were either conducive or detrimental to fostering their agency and grit for academic and professional goals. I have deliberately chosen to focus on the positives, in hopes that they will benefit those wishing to create positive environments for other children.

CHAPTER 4

The Social Environment and School Settings

As humans, we are ever-evolving. We reflect the relationship between the level of nurture we receive and the factors of nature and the environment we encounter regularly. In this chapter, I will focus on how a student's sense of self can improve through tailored support systems. Though each of my participants was forced to contend with some negative conditions associated with poverty, they all described the kinds of countering positive forces that helped them first realize, and then tap into, their potential. Specific influences guided them toward discovering *what* to be passionate about and allowed them to develop grit and agency over long periods. On a very basic level, this should be one of the major goals for schools and systems of education: to help each student recognize the many different pathways they could embark on, while empowering them to believe in themselves enough to follow the one that is most purposeful to them. Fostering a steadfast sense of hope is perhaps one of the best motivators for students and educators as we live up to collective responsibilities in education. Empowering and supporting students in this way is how schools could both nourish and construct a future society capable of tackling the many challenges—both social and individual—we all have ahead of us.

SOCIAL AND CULTURAL CAPITAL REVISITED: ESSENTIAL INGREDIENTS TO SUCCESS

Much of this chapter will focus on how young people learn to acquire social and cultural capital. Both forms of capital have real value in social environments through how they are leveraged in interactions with others. As I described in Chapter 2, social and cultural capital are similar to forms of currency used toward accessing opportunity. They have lifelong implications for students' ability to successfully navigate mainstream society and for them to develop and maintain meaningful relationships during their lives (Bourdieu, 1974; Lareau, 1987, 2002).

Horse to Water: Critical Thinking and Goal Formation

Sociologist Jay MacLeod's (1987) *Ain't No Makin' It* showed that action and determination alone could not improve the unfortunate predicaments of the young boys he studied. His longitudinal research demonstrated that in the absence of having procedural knowledge and the tangible social and cultural capital that is required to leverage agency (Patterson & Fosse, 2015), even positive thinking, rigorous personal effort, and intense investment in academics could not prevent "The Brothers" from reproducing their own families' lower-class positions (MacLeod, 1987). In other words, there are many factors beyond grit that students need to make it in the world.

Pierre Bourdieu (1986) said, "The convertibility of the different types of capital is the basis of the strategies aimed at [reproducing] capital" (p. 253). This statement is a bit convoluted but an important place to begin. As necessary as it is to convert certain types of capital into others to gain benefits, conversely, it is important to realize that some people also experience "invertability" (i.e., inability to convert or embody forms of capital), which can be a disadvantage. "Bob," a recent college graduate, described what it felt like to miss out on certain kinds of social and cultural capital growing up in the Bronx:

> I feel like a lot of the time in the community [where] I was raised, you're taught one way and you feel like that's the only one way there is. You know about the opportunities, but you don't see the way they can help you. They say, "Oh yeah! You can do this, and you can do that." But you don't see the value in the opportunity. I think most of the kids in my neighborhood don't see the long run.

Bob's words here highlight the real effects of capital on one's achievement mindset and worldview, and in his case his vantage point limited his conceptualization of opportunities available to him. If students have limited access to certain forms of capital, they may be less stimulated and less able to develop a specific (interest-based) plan for their future (Clausen & Jones, 1998; Shanahan et al., 2003).

To be able to survey potential opportunities and to prioritize which options to pursue requires critical thinking. For a person to decide what's best for them, they must recognize that certain choices would further their chances of self-improvement, which requires acknowledging that only certain opportunities will be most relevant to achieving particular goals. Bob mentions lacking this type of critical thinking, which may have kept him from developing the agency to pursue certain opportunities.

Tyrique, the participant I introduced in the Prologue, elaborates on this idea with a relevant and brilliant descriptive metaphor:

They say you can lead a horse to water, but you can't make it drink. But it's scarier when you lead a horse to water and they say, "What water?" I was the horse who didn't see the *ocean* in front of me. It's not a *conscious* decision. I [was] ignorant to the fact that what is in front of me is water.

When we talk about changes that we want to make to a system, it's with our understanding that these are *good* changes. But that may not be how it's interpreted. In every story, we have to understand that the person may not see that this is a *good* option. The person may actually not even understand that this is *water* that they're looking at.

When he was 22 years old, Tyrique got arrested for pulling an armed robbery while he held a full-time job at one of New York City's airports. He mentioned to me that even though he did not feel poor or that he needed money, because he was employed, he sometimes felt inadequate when thinking about his possibilities because he didn't go to college. Tyrique's friend group influenced him to participate in the robbery, which led to a 6-year imprisonment at Rikers Island and Green Haven Correctional Facility.

Tyrique's metaphor of not being able to see the water is directly tied to the ideas of capital and agency. At the time, to the 22-year-old Tyrique, the robbery seemed like a good option—a puddle of viable drinking water—amid, as he says, an "ocean" of other possibilities he could not see. While certain types of social and cultural capital can bridge a student's existing strengths, interests, and identity with those that we typically reward in mainstream society, if students are deprived of these bridges, they may fail to see how certain options are relevant or productive to them. It was not until being in prison, Tyrique said, through mentorship and other opportunities, that he started to recognize the true value of his existing level of education.

Sashko Danylenko

Cultural Competency: Respecting Personhood to Strengthen Views of Opportunity

Cultural competency is critical in helping students from diverse backgrounds, or those with disadvantages, to see the relevance and importance of academic opportunities. My findings extend the existing knowledge base that stresses the importance in teaching and mentorship of respecting a student's individuality, identity, and social position (Delpit, 2012; Duncan-Andrade & Morrell, 2008; Freire, 1968/1972). Through simple cultural sensitivity, actors in the lives of students help expand students' notions of all the possibilities in the world (Carter, 2003; Delpit, 2012; Ladson-Billings, 1997).

Before describing competence in school settings, allow me to expand on this notion just a bit more, using a story about everyday life. Alicia gave an example of how even her college friends, at her elite school, exhibit a lack of cultural competency:

> Last year, when I was doing my gingerbread house with my best friends, they were like, "Oh my god, how have you never made a gingerbread house before? That's crazy!" I told them I didn't have a childhood! And that's what I always tell my friends.

Remember that Alicia mentioned having "grown up too soon," not having the same comfortable childhood experiences that her friends did. Alicia told me that she was not at all offended by her friends' disbelief, but rather she knew that by simply assuming something about her, they showed the kind of subconscious errors that all of us are routinely capable of.

In the same vein as Alicia's story, I remember college students I have taught describing feeling alienated on the first day of class when professors ask about their summer vacations or what they did over break. While some students are able to travel around the world and visit exotic destinations, others simply cannot or might even be working to pay for their degrees. I learned from my students not to start my semester by asking about the kinds of luxuries we can easily forget not everyone has.

When teachers lack basic cultural competency, they can diminish a student's drive. Recall Joe, the young man who moved from New York City to live with his aunt in Edison, New Jersey, when he was a kid. The move allowed Joe to have much more stability and access to a better school. But one of his earliest and most formative memories of entering the new school system involves teachers who lacked cultural competency:

> In this new school, anytime something came up on Hispanics, my teacher would ask me for my opinion. I was, like, 13 years old. They put me on the spot. While back home in New York, I never had to worry about that, because everybody was [Hispanic].

Joe's teachers' singling him out and asking about Hispanic culture may have been an attempt to connect with him, but the efforts backfired. The teachers had not actually made an effort to get to know Joe on a personal basis, and by presuming to know where Joe came from, they ostracized him by calling unwanted attention to him in front of his classmates. Joe remembers mentally retreating in class instead of participating due to his teachers' approach.

Labeling Joe as the class expert and spokesperson on all things "Hispanic" instead of first seeing him as an individual, "just a kid" with his own experiences and stories, was culturally insensitive of his teachers. Boxing Joe into a preconceived notion was a subtle form of tokenization that many minority students, myself included, are all too familiar with. Similarly, it would be insensitive to ask a child about what family dinner is like at their house without first getting to know them; if a student were to come from a broken home with separated parents, or if they have experienced homelessness, like Joe had, they might immediately feel made to be an outsider. Again, these are common and easy mistakes, but we can avoid them over time if we are deliberate and determined to make these attitude and perspective shifts in ourselves.

While cultural incompetency can alienate students, the good news is that genuine cultural competency can motivate them through inclusion. Positive or beneficial cultural competency can come in different forms and can facilitate goal formation for students. For a visual, refer to my Conceptual Framework in Figures 1.2 and 1.3 in Chapter 1. "Cultural Competency" is located in the middle section. The competency can appear through the seemingly simple act of getting to know a student and their genuine interests.

"J-Stud" is a participant of mine who chose this alias because of his "emcee/rapper" name. Though I found him to be quite an outspoken young man, he told me that he wasn't always this way. Up until high school, J-Stud was shy and reserved and always sat in the back of his class with his head down. His English teacher noticed that every day he scribbled furiously in his notebook. This piqued her interest in him. Unlike others, he wasn't on his phone or sleeping. One day after class, she asked to see what he was writing, and he reluctantly showed her. She was surprised to find that his notebook was full of rap lyrics that were beautifully constructed, though not totally free from grammatical error. He continued the story:

> I wanted to do hip-hop music back then, really had a love for it, a passion for it, and that was the way I vented. I invent lyrics to get my frustration out. My teacher gave me the platform to express myself through good music. One of the stipulations was, "You have to go to class, J-Stud. You have to literally go to class in order for me to continue to work with you." She gave me the opportunity to go into an actual recording studio and put my music on a CD. I got

to perform in front of a bunch of students in a music class. I got a standing ovation. Having that mentor who is still very near and dear to me helped put me on the right track.

His teacher displayed one of the strongest forms of cultural competency that can motivate young people who need a little boost: she recognized various forms of his giftedness.[1] By realizing that J-Stud's affinity and talent for hip-hop could be an entry point toward raising his literacy and academic goals, his teacher used this as motivation. J-Stud's teacher offered to give him access to a recording studio where her friend worked *if* his attendance and grades improved. This moment was one of the most formative experiences in J-Stud's life; prior to this, he had been tracked into special education, and he used to resent school. This teacher helped him by not only boosting his confidence but also allowing him a tailored opportunity to slowly see the benefits of educational pursuits.

Having access to the recording studio changed the trajectory of J-Stud's life in an unexpected way. Not long thereafter, he was offered an internship there, which started a chain of turning-point events that led him down a path to pursue higher education. J-Stud also pivoted from his interest in music to finance, and today he is a director at a large investment bank in New York City. How did this come to be? We will revisit the impact of this chain of events in the last section of this chapter on "circle-jumping."

Strengthening Educational Attitudes

Simply telling students that they are capable is not enough to help. They need more in order to learn to display the kinds of behavior and thinking that will beget success out in the world. In schools, culturally *relevant* curricula is also needed to strengthen and improve students' existing worldview and act as a cultural bridge. Take for example this anecdote from "Imperial," the MPA candidate and Fulbright scholar in Europe. I asked him about his most memorable early experiences in school, those that shaped his motivation to excel academically. He replied:

> Overall, what really helped me was the fact that I went to a small, all-Black school in the Bronx. It was the last one in New York City. It closed down. It really influenced me. We learned about Black history, we learned about different Black innovators. We were taught from a young age, "You need to be like these people. You need to be as professional as them."

The various curricula Imperial describes helped to fortify his existing views of education and his perception of educational pursuit as beneficial, a general idea that is largely shared among many racial minorities from low-income backgrounds (Mickelson, 1990). Learning about Black individuals throughout history who excelled academically and professionally, and believing he could be like them, helped Imperial buy further into his education. These types of pedagogical approaches can counter the oversimplified idea that minorities might view educational opportunities as unfair and resist them (Ogbu, 1992).

Other participants shared sentiments about the importance of identifying with academic materials in order to then be moved by them. "Seku" told me that he had despised school as a child but said that what eventually changed his mind in young adulthood was finding the first book he connected with:

> I *hated* school. I *hated* reading. You couldn't get me to read a book. What changed my mind was that a close friend referred me to *The Autobiography of Malcolm X*. Once I read that, something triggered inside my head. I was 22. I was always aware of the names Malcolm X, Martin Luther King, Marcus Garvey, because these people are the names on the street signs. But I didn't know the effect these people had on our society. I started listening to [Malcolm's] speeches. I thought I had to do a lot better with my life. I got my GED, applied to college.

Seku began to see the importance of pursuing knowledge, and even educational credentials, from his ability to relate to the life of Malcolm X. I also find the mention of street signs incredibly significant. It is not enough for students to see the names of influential figures around them; they need the associated context to learn about the lives of these people to form a deeper connection to them.

Seku went on to tell me more of the reasons he felt a genuine connection with that book:

> Growing up in a household without a father and in a community where there are not too many positive male influences, I always wanted that growing up. I wanted to see a man I could follow. Reading Malcolm and seeing similarities—he grew up in a single-parent household since his father was murdered—he struggled, he hustled, he made sure his brother and sisters had something to eat. To see how he influenced the world, the Arab world, the Muslim world, how powerful he was, how good of a speaker he was, I wanted to do that. I started reading more. I became more frustrated with the way things are.

Similar to Tyrique, Seku was missing a positive male influence in his life. He found a literary role model in Malcolm X, and, slowly, his attitude about education, as well as his belief in himself, improved. He started pursuing knowledge from different outlets and applying what he was learning. Seku started to notice and become "frustrated with" the imperfections in his community. He created an after-school program based around civic engagement to address the problem of unsupervised youth in his neighborhood. In this program, youth and mentors read books like *The Autobiography of Malcolm X*. In a sense, Seku began to *positively* resist what he had come to see as normative conditions in his community, directly exercising his agency to create positive change (Rios, 2012). As discussed in Chapter 2, this type of positive resistance is a central component of agency and is particularly effective when a person first *reflects* on their social position and accordingly *acts* in the manner best suited to bring about the intended, improved outcome.

MENTORS AND NETWORKS: IMPROVING STUDENTS' WORLDVIEWS, SENSES OF SELF, AND HELP-SEEKING BEHAVIORS

The ability to see how education is relevant to one's trajectory benefits from experiences that connect a person's existing cultural capital to the types of capital that are typically rewarded in society. Though it is possible for students to connect with compelling educational material on their own, it is generally easier for them if mentors they can relate to deliver it through engaging curricula (Duncan-Andrade & Morrell, 2008). As Paulo Freire (1968/1972) contends, some label this a type of *critical* pedagogy, which I take to mean more necessary than analytical. Furthermore, when students connect to education through relationships that are based on mutual respect, there can be terrific long-term academic benefits. Imperial described the process through another example of a formative experience he had:

> We'd also have students from NYU teach us the SATs. They were students of color. They looked like us, they sounded like us, and they were in college doing big things. They were adults, they were cool, they were suave, and we wanted to be just like them. We didn't see that. I didn't see any kids from college or anything like that. Seeing these kids was amazing.

These mentors helped Imperial see himself in a more positive light. Through them, he realized his own potential to pursue higher education and fit in at environments he previously thought were very exclusive. His confidence (or self-efficacy) increased. He studied harder for the SAT with the specific goal of attending an elite college on scholarship like his older role models did. In essence, the NYU mentors provided Imperial with a type of mentor that some of my other participants, Tyrique and Seku, mentioned they wished they had had access to while growing up. Imperial illustrates the benefits of the cultural capital that he saw older students displaying: The way these students spoke and carried themselves resonated with him. Their ability to navigate smoothly across different social circles is what made Imperial want to "be just like them."

One reason students of color from low-income backgrounds may have a hard time seeing themselves in certain professions, such as teaching, could be that members of their communities are not well-represented in those jobs (Conchas, Lin, Oseguera, & Drake, 2015). New York City Department of Education (2019) initiatives such as NYC Men Teach, dedicated to hiring more men of color to teach within the New York City public school system, exemplify attempts to trim current race and gender gaps in the teaching force. And in California, the superintendent of public instruction, Tony Thurmond, identified hiring teachers of color, especially men, as one of his main priorities for his Closing the Achievement Gap Initiative in 2019. These efforts may have great payoffs: Seeing more people who look like them in front of the classroom may motivate more students to aspire to become teachers (Veiga, 2017). This can literally show minority students that there *is* a place for them in education and that there are benefits to going to school.

I tell groups of professionals with whom I speak about these topics that a mentor does not need to come from the same background nor be of the same race to help shape a young person's worldview and sense of self. One participant in my research project, "Willa," told me about an unexpected mentor in her life. Willa is one of those people who exudes warmth and kindness as soon as you meet her. She was a sophomore at an elite college when I met her for our interview, and she told me about a male nurse who shaped her career goals after her mother had just passed away from cancer. Willa had always wanted to be a doctor, but because of her experience with this man, she later decided to switch to nursing. I asked her about what caused this shift in perspective and goals:

> I wrote my Common App essay on this. I was inspired to be a nurse by my mom's hospice nurse, actually. After she passed away, my whole family said, "Willa, you've got to be a doctor. You've got the smarts." Still, I knew I would get the most clarity out of life if one day I could be a mom and the type of mom that my mom was with me. I really couldn't do that if I was an MD. As she was starting to pass away, the hospice nurse was always there. Not only doing procedural things but also emotional things. He made every moment there simple and special. He would sit with me on the bed with her while she was unconscious. We talked together, we cried together. It felt right. So, what can I do in the medical field, since I love science and helping people, while also fulfilling the role of mommy that I want?

It goes without saying that young people can be incredibly impressionable. And if you're going to influence someone, coming from a place of kindness can create immeasurable, positive change for their future. Unknowingly, the hospice nurse had a very direct hand in Willa's career path. Now enrolled in an extremely well-respected nursing program, Willa says that it would be difficult to balance her goals of being a loving mother and a successful career woman if she had pursued an MD instead of the nursing degree.

Willa, who consistently demonstrated a tremendous amount of grit (she applied to 18 colleges while living at her aunt's house after her mother passed away), also developed the foresight that she would not have much time for family as a doctor. Her ability to combine critical thinking with focused effort exemplifies having agency. Agency is about following a very specific, goal-oriented pathway while being mindful of potential challenges or changes in circumstances. The hospice nurse helped Willa see her future self in a new light while also providing basic care and emotional support. At the outset, they did not seem to share much in common, but they were able to connect over mutual interests of science and Willa's desire to go into medicine. Willa's interactions with the nurse helped her visualize another path to practice medical care and also be an attentive mother one day.

Genuine connection based on mutual respect is the defining quality of a successful mentor–mentee relationship. On a theoretical level, this means that tapping into students' existing forms of social or cultural capital can promote critical thinking and allow educators to help students recognize their social position and the structures in their lives to be transformed (Freire, 1968/1972). Strengthening a young person's educational attitudes also increases their sense of self and fosters agency as students continue to assess their potential to form new and better goals themselves. Tyrique's story exemplifies the importance of practicing cultural competency in effective mentorship. During our interview, Tyrique said that being raised by a single mother made him feel like he was missing a male role model in his life and that this might have made him more impressionable when it came to his friends, many of whom ended up being negative influences:

All in high school, anytime I needed any type of fatherly figure support or advice, I got that from my peers. They were older than me, so I felt that there was validity in what they were saying.

Even though Tyrique had a stable job, he was swayed by his peers into thinking that robbing someone rich would be a good idea. He had closed himself off from the idea that he could receive mentorship from someone older and more mature. Not growing up with a dad in the picture made Tyrique used to the idea that he'd have to fend for himself. This mindset continued into Tyrique's sentence at Rikers Island, until a critical moment, which he described to me:

> My first year, although it wasn't what I wanted, I hung around the same character type of people: people who weren't looking to progress themselves. I was around some dangerous people, man. Making stupid choices, carrying weapons. About a year into my incarceration, there was a guy who had done a tremendous amount of time, running a college program. I didn't realize what the value of college was. He told me, "You're going down this road I've been on 10 times already, and it never ends well."

The older man stuck his neck out and showed interest in Tyrique—something that not many other men had done for him before, or at least not in a productive manner. The man offered Tyrique an opportunity to join him and work on a youth mentoring project because he noticed Tyrique had a knack for mentoring younger detainees. Tyrique, 22 years old at the time, was initially startled by the offer. He even felt angry at times. "What are you trying to be, my father? You're not going to resolve my daddy issues," Tyrique told me jokingly, replaying his conversation with the man. However, the older man remained patient and understanding. Tyrique described that the man asked him if he wanted to be a part of the problem or a part of the solution. That question stayed with Tyrique for over a decade. The man did not tell Tyrique what to do but instead verbalized the two main options Tyrique had, one of which would hopefully put him on a much better path than staying on the one he was on. Eventually this not-too-overbearing approach helped Tyrique decide to join the mentorship program.

Tyrique went on to explain that his new mentor became influential in his life because he respected and genuinely understood where Tyrique came from. They had similar experiences growing up, and his mentor had also been caught up in a string of misfortunes and poor decisions. He was serving a life sentence as a result. He simply wanted to help Tyrique out of real empathy. Tyrique could relate to him as an example of what could befall him if he did not turn things around and seek self-improvement. Some research finds that strategies—such as recruiting men of color to go into teaching in public schools—that enable students to better relate to their mentors, turning otherwise unfamiliar individuals into role models, can expand students' sense of self and worldview (Karcher, 2008). The theme of mentorship was conducive to Tyrique's eventual decision to pursue a college degree while in prison. Tyrique mentioned that receiving guidance from his new mentor, as well as his own mentorship of younger incarcerated men, led him to the desire to advance his own education.

Tyrique's relationship with his mentor is an example of cultural competency because the older man understood how best to approach Tyrique.

Cultural competence implies having a level of respect and understanding for another's personhood and background—something that I believe everyone should exhibit, especially teachers, because of the impact they make on students' lives. There is an unspoken burden for students of all backgrounds to integrate into a middle-class environment or dominant culture, but there is an important opportunity in education to redistribute that burden and create supports that help all students feel welcomed and appreciated regardless of where they come from.

A year after joining the mentorship program, Tyrique decided to enroll in the prison college program. He explains that one of the most memorable and transformative events he experienced was in his new religious studies course:

> The best thing I got out of it was the ability to do college-level work. That was something I'd never seen myself doing. When I got my first A, I questioned my professor afterward. "Why'd you give me this A?" I thought that she was being nice. *We're in prison, so she's being easy on us.* She said, "No, Tyrique, I gave you that A because it was a good paper." It was one of those moments that I look back on in my incarceration where my empowerment just grew.

In this story, we hear about how Tyrique's attitude toward education grew more positive as he started to see himself as truly capable of scholarly pursuits (Mickelson, 1990). Tyrique's previous experiences in education had left him questioning his real academic potential, so his decision to pursue a college degree was a brave one, and it was validated by this single experience. In his mind, there was no way he deserved the A, but this teacher assured Tyrique that he had in fact earned it. The high expectations of his teacher fostered Tyrique's desire to keep taking more college courses. Eventually, he left prison with nearly three years of college credits.

"Help-Seeking" Behavior

When individuals see their new skills begetting new rewards, they typically want to maintain these gains and keep practicing. I found that people celebrate the fruits of their networking labors in this way. J-Stud told me that he keeps a detailed record of his expanding network. I followed up by asking if he kept a spreadsheet with mentors and new contacts, and he replied:

> I actually draw my network out. I put "network" in the middle and then put little lines to say, "I know this person that works here." I want to continue to expand my network, by adding two or three people a year.

Honestly, this quote from J-Stud is what allowed me to visualize the concept of circle-jumping in the first place. By expanding his own network and seeing how beneficial that has been, J-Stud developed a more formal method for charting this process. Some of my readers might find this to be a tad obsessive or even perhaps a bit superficial, but they have to realize that when a person does not have readily available "silver spoon" connections in their lives to help get them opportunities, they have to work harder and smarter. J-Stud got positive reinforcement and the confidence he needed to succeed at work by actively seeking help from those with more experience in his field.

One of the results is that J-Stud expresses his gratitude by mentoring others, a form of service akin to the kind of civic duty I discussed in Chapter 2. Recognizing the supports that helped him find his path to a career has led him to reciprocate in two different settings: he gives support and guidance to new employees and minority team members at the investment bank where he works, and he is also a role model to youth in his community. In these ways, we can see that both agency and grit have reproducible effects because the agency his teachers and mentors cultivated also gave way to grit and a long-term, fixated view of goal-setting and achieving.

Recall JLo, the "larger than life" man who was also my oldest participant. He applied a similar type of formal relationship-making to his college experience. He told me that the younger college students looked up to him and often asked for advice about life. The handful of JLo's peers who came to say hi to him during our interview are a testament to the tremendous potential of networking in college, even through something as simple as making friends. I asked him what he tells these students who look up to him, and he replied:

> I tell everybody this: College is a learning experience; it's one big social experiment. It's not what you know, it's *who* you know. Someone you have a basic stats class with today could be the person who has a great job tomorrow. They could hook you up! Don't be that wallflower in the corner. No one will forget about me because I'm in your face. If the person interviewing you doesn't think they can be next to you for 40 hours a week, they need to know they can at least be comfortable around you. And as big and as ugly as I am, I think people can be comfortable with me.

It is worth mentioning that JLo is not only a large man with a charmingly loud demeanor but also visibly blind in one eye from a violent injury some years ago. His blind eye is sure to catch anyone's attention at first glance. But, true to himself, JLo brings levity to the situation, as he does in the previous quote. In each college class, JLo worked to cultivate relationships with fellow students and professors. He believes these relationships work best if they are mutually beneficial so that people can help to grow each other's strengths. JLo used college to grow not just his own agency but the agency of his fellow classmates. The positive reinforcement of his help-seeking tendencies fueled his sense of purpose as well—an idea I will elaborate on in Chapter 5.

Circle-Jumping: Navigating from Network to Network

It is well documented in education research that youth from lower-income backgrounds often feel less entitled to ask questions and participate actively in some social and formal settings (Lareau, 2002), but when students are offered forms of capital that are easily applicable to their lives, they can learn to tap into these important skills as needed. In particular, students who develop stronger communication and relational skills through mentor–mentee relationships often can leverage forms of cultural capital in effective networking practices. When J-Stud's teacher gave him access to a recording studio in high school, she started a chain reaction that would open many more doors for him. Throughout our interview, J-Stud mentioned that he has developed and almost perfected his ability to network just from that initial opportunity granted to him by his teacher. I asked him what he credits for developing this skill, to which he said:

> I'm always seeking out mentors, trying to learn something from somebody in a senior position, or just trying to get a different perspective or words of encouragement. Being able to tell my story and have people say, "J-Stud. You know what? It sounds like you've been through a lot, but you've persevered. I like that about you. Stay in touch and let me know how I can help you."

J-Stud is a prime example of how effective mentorship can foster students' continued development of help-seeking behavior so that they can learn to be comfortable in various environments. Help-seeking behavior may sound like an oversimplified term for an extremely necessary component to success. Imagine that the opposite of it is feeling excluded, dejected, and uninterested in participating in formative events and/or groups, and behaving in a way that reflects these feelings. Both of these—help-seeking and its opposite—can become habitual behaviors based on the influences a student has. Mentorship can act as the greatest positive reinforcement for students beyond academic settings. (This is part of the reason that after-school programs can be so impactful in a young person's life.) From his high school English class, J-Stud learned the importance of making the best of each opportunity and how to treat life experiences as building blocks to get from one goal to the next. This is, in essence, how he went from being a failing high school student, to pursuing his associate's degree, to earning his bachelor's degree while simultaneously maintaining a job in the financial sector.

J-Stud exemplifies a process that I have come to call circle-jumping. Circle-jumping is an action-oriented, simplified perspective on how networks and social mobility might work. The process allows people to navigate from one network to another, signaling their gains in cultural capital along the way, as they tap into new social circles that increase their social capital. All the while, in an ideal process, a person's ability to visualize their goals and strategize ways to achieve them increases.

Circle-jumping is fairly easy to depict visually. In Figure 4.1, the large central circles each represent a network that J-Stud was in at some point in his life. The small spokes that are connected to the large circle each represent a person in J-Stud's life who helped shape his identity, experiences, and access to resources in that environment. The relationships between people in the different network circles can help to create the connective links that allow J-Stud to move between the networks. Through these links, J-Stud is introduced to new networks, where he can meet new people, learn new skills, acquire additional cultural capital, and gain access to additional networks. For instance, his English teacher helped put J-Stud in touch with a recruiter at the recording studio, which led to J-Stud obtaining an internship there. Later on, the accountant at the recording studio internship connected him to the internship coordinator at the investment bank, where he was able to get his first full-time job.

Figure 4.1. Circle-Jumping: A Model on How Individuals Navigate Between Networks and Build Social Capital

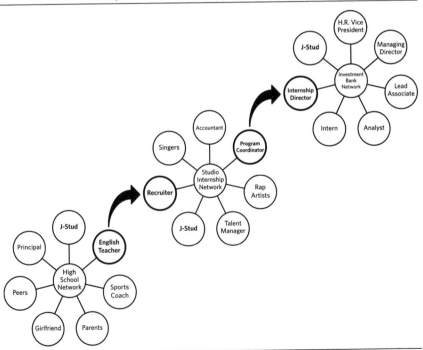

As shown in recent research on students and their access to networks, who students know is immeasurably important in the internship and career opportunities that befall them (Fisher, 2018). Not only that, but most people end up working at least somewhere in their lives (often their first jobs) due to having a strong connection to someone already working there. This has bleak implications for students who grow up with less access to professional networks, like the ones Bob mentioned having in the Bronx. Bob's example justifies the importance of social or human capital in the most basic of forms; though all students would benefit from having a strong mentor in their lives, sometimes even being in the presence of impressive, role-model-type adults (having access to see these individuals operate in their daily lives) is enough for a student to imagine the different beneficial outcomes their life could take.

These circles help individuals imagine and visualize new goals and teach them how to conduct themselves in the next circle. As a high school student, J-Stud met multiple people at the studio while recording there. He ended up getting an internship, which he renewed for 2 years while also pursuing his associate's degree. Interacting with the studio's accountant fostered a passion for finance in J-Stud. He began learning about the economics of the music industry, which led him to earn his associate's degree in financial services. The degree helped earn him another internship, this time at an investment bank.

The investment banking internship motivated J-Stud to earn his bachelor's degree because most of his peers there had four-year degrees. Keeping a foot in the bank while going to school allowed him to be hired full-time after he completed his bachelor's. Without the initial circle and opportunities provided by his high school teacher, social mobility almost certainly would not have been possible for J-Stud. His experiences in each individual circle helped to increase his own awareness of his goals and what steps he would need to take in order to achieve them.

As a testament to how agency can be contagious, J-Stud chooses to live in Jamaica, Queens, where he grew up. He does this despite having a longer commute. He hopes to serve as an example for the youth in his community. In essence, J-Stud is one of those "spokes" from the diagram in Figure 4.1, a presence in the neighborhood, one that may help other neighborhood kids realize their own potential to jump from circle to circle and climb as they find fulfilling and purposeful work in their lives. He also serves as a testament to the idea that you don't have to leave your neighborhood, or where you grow up, to "make it" in the world.

Maybe one of the most beneficial aspects of circle-jumping is that an individual can improve various skills by building off previous improvement areas. The "jumping" implies navigating between different social circles, picking up useful cultural codes in each one, and using them to propel oneself toward another circle of higher status. Sunny mentioned how his experience in an after-school program helped him to visualize someday working in finance:

> I would attribute a lot [to the after-school program]. The sense that I wanted to be successful, that was inherent. But knowing how to frame success in different avenues, I didn't understand. I didn't know what investment banking was until I went to [the after-school program]. That provided me with an intuition. At an investment bank, I was around *elites* that went to prestigious schools. I was able to say, "This is what success looks like. I don't have to be a musician or be in the streets. I can obtain this by going to school and learning the mannerisms and how to move." Investment banking and management consulting . . . it's about who's smart. It's about how you dress, how you talk. How does your resume line up? How does your story line up? And that's what [the program] taught me.

Sunny's after-school program helped him channel his existing strengths and motivations into the financial arena. He started to learn the codes needed to excel in this work environment. As a kid, he had a relatively limited perception of the different avenues he could take toward achieving the prosperity he knew he wanted, but connecting with the professionals who mentored him in the after-school program helped Sunny learn how to interact with different bankers. He calls this a type of "intuition," one that certain people pick up more naturally given the networks they have access to. But this perspective could also be considered as gains in existing cultural and social capital. Each of Sunny's networks influenced his development and his ability to propel himself to the next circle he sought to be a part of.

CONCLUSION

It is important to restate that formal education systems can actually serve to reproduce the existing patterns of inequality they strive to dismantle. This is too challenging a reality for schools to confront by themselves because they are at the mercy of many socioeconomic constraints (reflecting the economic, social, and cultural capital of their parents, students, and teachers). Additionally, because so much of a child's development takes place outside of school, away from formal schooling, it is important for stakeholders in the lives of youth to have a robust view of what students' lives are really like to understand where they need more support as well as to imagine what they are capable of. These are the foundations of genuine relationships that can work as entry points to connecting with students and motivating them.

For educators, a place to start building relationships and promoting a student's growth is thinking about what it will take for a student to develop autonomy. It may sound counterintuitive to a degree, that helping a student to become self-sufficient is one of the foundations of the teacher–student relationship. Yet that element is what will allow the teacher to step aside one day and let the student flourish. I will reiterate this in the book's Conclusion, but allowing students to play an active, intentional, and potentially leading role in their own learning is important in ensuring that they continue to develop a sense of autonomy. To encourage agency-building, teachers should work to ensure that at every step a student can answer these questions:

- What exactly am I trying to learn here, and why?
- What are the different ways I can show that I have learned or mastered this?
- What is the next thing I should then be able to conquer?
- And if I get stuck, how can I locate the resources I need for help?

This chapter reviewed how my participants conceive and embody their various roles in different social environments. Interacting successfully with others in various academic and professional settings requires training and practice. It is incredibly important to be mindful of the lasting and real effects that social and cultural capital have in individuals' lives. They are important concepts to keep in mind for people who care about students, to think beyond the concrete and visible markers of the financial means people have. Social and cultural capital each stem from a person's realities, shaping their unique understanding of the world. I have provided examples of how both social capital (through mentors and networks) and cultural capital (through cultural competency and culturally relevant curricula) can help students learn to think critically and subsequently form relevant goals.

My participants mentioned that mentors who were cognizant of where they came from were the most impactful. The mentors who respected participants' personalities, interests, and inherent forms of giftedness connected with them best. Those who may have reached out in more superficial ways—like Joe's teacher who called him out to represent Hispanic culture—were not effective. As Tyrique explained, the right forms of support help a horse to recognize that there is water in the first place and then helps the horse learn to drink it.

Tyrique told me the story of when he reconnected with his mentor very briefly in the midst of a prison transition:

He had no idea how much he had changed my life. I brought him all of my certificates. I was telling him like, "Yo, you literally and drastically changed the way that I saw myself." I showed him the stuff I did. You know what's crazy? At this point, he got choked up, and he said, "Holy shit. You just go every day, and you throw seeds. And you don't know what's going to happen to those seeds."

Tyrique had moved from Rikers Island to Green Haven Correctional at that point and had lost touch with the influential man in his life. It was only at Green Haven that he began taking college courses, so his mentor did not realize how much their interactions had set Tyrique on an improved path until Tyrique was able to tell and show him directly. Tyrique told me that the man became emotional hearing about his successes. Sometimes *educators* may not realize the important ways in which they help shape how their students see themselves.

In some cases, people once actively disengaged from school are able to educate and motivate themselves into academic pursuits through locating culturally relevant curricula, as Seku did upon reading about Malcolm X. When there are mentors who display cultural competency or who provide students with culturally relevant curricula and educational materials, students can better see themselves in a variety of social roles, many of which they previously did not realize were available to them.

Finally, one of the culminating effects of having these kinds of beneficial supports is gaining the ability to network skillfully and to exhibit continued help-seeking behavior. These basic traits are critical as people strive to move up the social ladder and enter different social networks, as portrayed in my circle-jumping subtheme. JLo eloquently explained this idea:

> A closed mouth does not get fed. You always got to talk to people and find out what resources are at your disposal and seek out help when you need help. Don't be too proud. I ask for help from everybody.

JLo realizes that asking for help is not easy; sometimes pride can be a roadblock, and often students of color or those from lower-income homes may not necessarily have been raised in ways conducive to feeling entitled to ask for help (Lareau, 2002). These students sometimes have to actively learn these abilities for themselves, which requires both practice and guidance. Herein lies an additional problem with making claims that some students may embody deficient behaviors (perhaps isolating themselves in class) or trying to highlight that these students come from deficient home cultures: The premise simply reinforces the notion that some students are deficient in the experiences they have been afforded in life. However, in this chapter I have shown that when the right support systems or experiences are provided to these students, there are highly beneficial and lasting effects that create academic and professional excellence.

CHAPTER 5

The Ever-Evolving Human

To me, one of the most powerfully moving things in my study has been realizing that people who have experienced immense challenges often have a heightened ability to perceive the kinds of changes they wish to see in the world. From having grown up in challenging circumstances, individuals like my participants may have a heightened understanding of the problems in their communities that need to be addressed. They may also have innovative ideas for fixing the kinds of structural barriers they experienced.

As such, the goal of this last chapter on my study's findings is to further amplify the voices of my participants. Often, individuals do not receive a platform to express their views in the very research that assesses the types of situations they have actually experienced firsthand (Heckman, 1995; hooks, 1992; Morrell, 2004). I hope I have made some space for these sometimes absent perspectives of underrepresented students in education research. This process has allowed me to learn how individuals can move from being disenfranchised and disengaged in academic settings, to taking control of constructs that affect their lives. "The Ever-Evolving Human" presents the factors my participants explicitly identified as key to their continued development and ongoing journeys to finding success and happiness.

The themes in this chapter stem from what was almost directly said by participants. Some of the headings that follow are phrases directly taken from the interviews I conducted. Responses related to purpose and mental health and happiness were particularly prominent, and I have extracted some of the most important elements from them for you here.

In earlier chapters, I mention that one of the challenges low-income students of color can face is learning how to develop *specific* visions for how to recognize and access opportunities available to them. I describe how factors like tailored mentorship and culturally respectful educational materials can help students develop and cultivate passions over the long term. Interestingly, in her book *Grit*, Duckworth mentions that developing a passion is difficult not only for students with financial disadvantages but for many others as well. She says, "I don't think most young people need encouragement to follow their passion. Most would do exactly that—in a heartbeat—if they only had a passion in the first place" (Duckworth, 2016, p. 99).

This chapter will extend the idea of purpose and examine more ways in which individuals internally form and pursue goals. The themes described will relate specifically to the idea of passion—how it can be fueled, maintained, and also lost and then regained. A major goal for individuals and students looking to better themselves is to realize that the search for passion is an ongoing one; to truly home in on something fulfilling as a guiding light requires actively creating and immersing oneself in the right ecosystems with the needed supports that will help to encourage, validate, and enhance those very efforts.

PURPOSE: A COMPONENT OF PASSION
AND A BASIS FOR DEVELOPING GRIT AND AGENCY

The idea of having a purpose has been a driving force in my participants' lives and their success. Without purpose, these individuals would not be able to fully exercise their agency, like having a boat but lacking a motor. Similarly, purpose is documented in grit research as being one of the components of passion that then leads to the formulation of grit. In *Grit*, Duckworth (2016) says, "Interest is one source of passion. Purpose—the intention to contribute to the well-being of others—is another. The mature passions of gritty people depend on both" (p. 143). I love this definition of purpose that Duckworth puts forward. I find it uniquely compelling because we tend to think about purpose only as it relates to someone's desired objectives or the reasons behind taking any action.

In today's world, self-interest seems to reign supreme, which may cause our idea of purpose to rarely be tied to contributing to "the well-being of others," as Duckworth puts it. However, my research aligns with hers; my participants care tremendously about others, constantly expressing their desires to give back to their communities and engage in other, various forms of altruism. Perhaps we are much more deeply socially integrated and interdependent than we realize. To add to Duckworth's definition of purpose, my research would simply add that purpose also often entails a process of reimagining and retooling one's hopes for the future. Purpose is a process, and thus it is not stagnant; treating purpose as an achievable end is not productive.

GIVING BACK TO MAKE POSITIVE CHANGE:
A FORM OF POSITIVE RESISTANCE

Most of my participants expressed an undying desire to help other people. When I asked about future ambitions and goals, 70% of participants ($n = 35$) explicitly stated that they are driven to help others in their life's endeavors. Many connected service to their occupational calling, and others mentioned that service is a life philosophy. Here are several variations of this sentiment:

"Paying it forward is really important to me and drives me to do this type of work." (Roxanne)

"What about becoming a doctor appeals to me? Helping people. And I know it sounds cliché." (Rose)

"I want to continue to set an example that others can follow. Not just my children but also my children's circle of friends." (JLo)

"I'm thinking that if even a busy man has time for other people, why not help others? I really do believe that no man is an island. We survive because we help each other." (Brian)

"For me, I don't feel that it's about the money. I just want to help people. And I think that the higher up you go, or the more established you are, it's a better chance you have of helping people." (Esquire)

An overwhelming number of participants connected the idea of helping others to success. Forty-one participants (82%) made statements about how helping others was important to them. Thirty-eight (76%) articulated a desire to pursue a profession that would allow them to help people for a living. These answers came up when I asked very broad questions such as, "Right now, what is most important to you in life?" or "What are some of the things that drive you?" The career goals I noted included wanting to become a teacher (Stan, Sasha, Chris, Nadira), a lawyer (Esquire, Joe, Jon), a forensic psychologist (Winchester), and a health care professional (Willa), or imply wanting to work in policy (Tyrique, Mario, Gouvia, Imperial) to serve others.

By pulling a bit outward from some of the previous statements, we can see the level of intent in the desire to help others. Alicia a bit jokingly mentioned that she needed to get her "life together" before being able to help others. I asked her, "In what sense?" She replied:

I want to be an educator. I want to have a hand in education reform and education policymaking. I have a lot of intersections that interest me. For one, I have a huge interest in incarceration education. Well, I'm a prison abolitionist. I don't think prisons should exist in the first place. I want to abolish the American criminal justice system, and we can create something else that is judicial in its place. But, since it does still exist, being able to educate those who have been formerly incarcerated, and make education accessible to them, is something I'm interested in. Schools should cater to the students they serve. I say serve because it is the role of these educational institutions to serve their students and to serve their community, not the other way around. A lot of schools aren't doing that. My high school didn't do that. Those are the kind of things I want to change.

Alicia uses her own experiences to inform her future plans. She believes that her high school did not effectively *serve* the many other low-income students who went there. The goals she describes here involve creating change on both micro and macro levels, at the person-to-person level of being an educator and at the policy reform level. And yet Alicia connects these ideas coherently, expressing a resentment and resistance toward the current system of mass incarceration and connected educational systems that are failing students.

Similarly, "Rose" mentions the idea of changing systems as a motivation behind her goal of becoming a doctor.

What about becoming a doctor appeals to me? Helping people. And I know it sounds cliché. But last summer I raised money for a mission trip in the [Dominican Republic]. That was my first trip there. I went and worked at a government-run hospital. I started buying supplies in bulk, asking people for donations. Five bucks here, 10 bucks there. I ended up raising a little over a thousand. I was able to buy blood pressure cuffs, Band-Aids, kid's Tylenol, Advil, stuff like that. I shipped it.

My original plan was to donate to the hospital that I was working in, but once I got there, I realized the politics—all those efforts wouldn't have been properly administered and used the way I wanted. I talked to people. Where I was, the poverty was insane. I'd talk to people and go to the big stash and make a little box of whatever they needed. I'd go to their house, and I'd give it to them so the supplies could be used the way I wanted. For the people who needed it.

Rose also describes wanting to change social problems by participating in grassroots efforts. By collecting medical supplies and then distributing them to needy families firsthand, Rose resisted the Dominican health care structures, which she saw as corrupt. She had first answered my question by saying that becoming a doctor would allow her to be in a position to help people, but as she elaborated, she showed the many small-scale efforts she had already undertaken to be of service to others. By recognizing a problem and implementing her own, hands-on solution, Rose displayed a significant amount of both grit and agency. Doing so on her first trip to the Dominican Republic, where her grandparents grew up, helped Rose form a deeper connection to her family history and to her Dominican identity.

Multiple participants explicitly connected their future career goals and desire to help others to the disadvantages and struggles they personally faced; for many more of the participants, that logic was implied. For example, both Seku and Imperial, who had negative and unsafe experiences growing up in public housing, described wanting to work in housing development. They aspire to be on the front lines by creating and providing safe, affordable housing options for their communities.

Playing devil's advocate, I asked Alicia why she would want to aid others when she grew up underprivileged. I asked her why she wouldn't look after her own success and wealth first. She replied emphatically:

> Because it's not fair! How dare I? I've had to house some of my friends when they weren't able to pay the light or water bills. I can't be over here acting like I'm going to [business school] to become a Wall Street banker. How dare I? That's not okay. My mother is a cafeteria worker. She gets $10 an hour. Her annual salary is under poverty.
>
> How dare I? Like, sure I can use my millions and buy both my parents nice houses and cars, but that's not paying *everyone's* light and water bills. And then again, let's say I did take these millions and as a philanthropist I threw this money at this community. Threw it at the schools and threw it at the parks and the rec center. It can be helpful, but it creates this type of dependency structure. Like, you know, money is great and it's useful but it's also important to be self-generating. Getting money is not going to eradicate poverty. Eradicating poverty is going to eradicate poverty.

It is safe to say that by the end of our interview I was in awe of this college student. Her desire to assist others seems to first come from knowing how difficult life can be for some people. Alicia's repetition of "How dare I?" has stuck with me over time. She emphasizes that she needs to personally help to bring about the social changes she wants to see. Connecting this discovery to my earlier finding that some individuals feel robbed of childhood from increased early responsibilities, it's clear that some students continuously walk around with heavy, often invisible burdens on their shoulders. Sometimes the weight of these is equal to feeling responsible to lift up an entire community by oneself.

Alicia also shows great maturity in understanding that simply giving money to charities and community-minded organizations will not bring about the structural changes we need to address and eliminate many problems. I found this to be a particularly interesting take. For one, it sounds oddly similar to arguments that conservatives might make against the welfare state, which goes to show that one person can exhibit multiple nuanced views on the various policies that may or may not work in our society. Boxing someone into a preconceived notion of their identity and value systems only serves to superficially separate us and is counterintuitive to progressive dialogue. Instead Alicia, through her own agency, wants to foster the agency of others. All of my participants have demonstrated a level of appreciation for their own journeys, with a reflexive ability to look back at where they once were, appreciate where they are now, and plan for where they are heading. As such, purpose in one's pursuits, sometimes through selflessness, is closely tied to agency as well.

FAITH: REAFFIRMS PURPOSE, HONES FOCUS, AND FUELS AGENCY

Related to purpose is the concept of faith, or a persistent belief in something larger than oneself. I find that for my participants, having faith is connected to optimism and confidence, and faith has helped many of the individuals in this study to feel more sanguine and prepared to deal with the adverse circumstances they faced. One-fourth of my participants mentioned that either faith or religion played a large role in their lives. Seku, who was raised as a Jehovah's Witness but now practices Islam, related the idea of faith and belief in a higher power to his ability to find solutions and think positively. He said:

> Faith and religion play a key role for me. I feel like I've been helped a lot. I haven't had the hardest road to travel, when compared to other people. Who am I to complain? There's always solutions—everything has a solution. Even when I'm weak or I feel like I didn't do enough and failed, I feel like it's okay because I'll do better tomorrow. I got air in my lungs, I'm breathing. I got my kid next to me and family. That's what I focus on if I have negative thoughts.

I find it astonishing that Seku, who was once homeless and trying to maintain his hygiene by washing up in public restrooms, says he hasn't traveled the "hardest road" compared to others. Stan shares a sentiment similar to this when answering my question about how he prevents difficulties in his life from inhibiting him. He stated that "belief" is what helps him stay positive:

> I think it's belief. You have to believe. There are times when you beat yourself up and you don't believe. But faith, whether through religion or not, helps the knowing that one day it will get better. For example, it rained all day last week. But today it got better. You have to take

advantage of a day like this. You get up and you fight. It takes fight and it takes grit. A lot of people like to focus on the negative and like to downplay what could happen. A lot of people are afraid of success. It's like people who like to argue in relationships because they're not used to being happy. Something had to construct this world to function so perfectly. And for them to do what they did, people also need to think they have a purpose and look to find it.

At this point, the reader might be wondering if the folks I research ever get to rest. To be honest, I'm not so sure that they do. Stan almost sounds like a boxer, connecting the concept of faith to his seemingly ceaseless grit, claiming that having faith and deciding to work hard every day requires effort and tenacity. Even though it can take a real effort to get out of bed every morning, these participants mention doing so from an underlying confidence that their efforts will prove worthy over time. Faith can motivate people to remain regimented about self-improvement by bringing a positive outlook on life. At the same time, self-improvement can be exhausting, and ceaseless grit can take a toll. We will revisit this idea shortly in the section to follow on burnout.

It seems that faith is useful in finding purpose, staying positive, and then harnessing grit. Tyrique told me that during his life in prison he felt a desire for discipline, which emerged around the same time that he discovered Islam:

> I was upstate for about a year, and I was maturing. I was changing physically, I was changing mentally, emotionally, physically, and spiritually. This idea of maturation had reached such a point where I started to evolve as a man in general. I made a conversion to Islam and thought, "You know what? To do this program I need discipline in my life."
>
> Before I was very undisciplined and that had [led] me to make bad decisions. Growing up, if someone asked me, what was Islam, I could not even begin to even tell you. But in prison one of my very close friends was Muslim and practicing. He had told me about Ramadan and fasting, and I asked, "How do you do that? That's insane. I don't think I could do that." I had all of these questions, and I became very intrigued and very focused on implementing discipline in my life. Of course, Islam is a very disciplined religion. That appealed to me, and then college appealed to me. The next thing you know, I say yes to this guy who pushed me through the program.

The disciplinary nature of Islamic faith appealed to Tyrique as he matured into a young adult. His desire to improve himself spurred his desire to convert, and his newfound faith helped him to stay on track and make good decisions. Religion provided Tyrique a structure that he did not find in his community or at home. It allowed him to create an infrastructure that he needed to progress himself. These practices went hand-in-hand with the academic pursuits that were also on Tyrique's mind. Discipline via Islam and faith contributed immensely to Tyrique's decision to join the prison's college education program.

I find that faith and/or religion can offer tangible support to those who have challenges. Faith may or may not be explicitly tied to a religion; however, the institutions (e.g., churches, temples, mosques) and rituals (e.g., prayer, meditation, fasting) of organized religion can enhance a person's connectedness to others and to the human experience (Durkheim, 1912/2008). One of the most beneficial aspects of religion that my participants mentioned revolved around having structured networks and organized communities of support. Liz connected this idea of structure back to her desire to help others:

> A big part of my childhood and teenage years was I was part of a church. I was helping a lot there. I helped teach an English class to Spanish-speaking adults. I did simple things, like plan menus to sell certain food on Sunday to fundraise money for different events. Being in that environment and being able to do something as simple as [giving] up your chair for an older lady, and to see their smile on their face, that's nice.

Church gives Liz a place to be of service to others. She goes regularly because of the sense of community she finds there. Her church taught her important skills like how to teach adults. And when Liz was placed under academic probation in her first year of college (which I will elaborate on in the next section), friends from her church helped her to get back on track and reenroll.

One of the most interesting things that I have learned about faith and purpose is that a simple but unwavering belief in something "greater" or "higher" helps people with their day-to-day difficulties and encourages general happiness. "Winchester," one of my most mentally disciplined participants—a 24-year-old, married Marine who wakes up at 5:00 every morning—says that faith enabled him to steer himself back to productivity and away from negative influences. After a markedly turbulent time between his parents, Winchester started rebelling until he began to rediscover his faith:

> I just kept rebelling against my mother. But for some reason, I ended up going back to church one day. Actually, my mom started going back to church when my mother and father started fixing their relationship. Whenever I go to church, I want to feel comfortable. So

one day, my mother was going to church and said, "Do you want to come with me?" I went with some teenage youth group, and thought, "This feels nice." I had this anger and this hatred inside of me, and going back to church lifted that away. Practically . . . I went back to God from having questioned my faith. I used to be mad about the things I couldn't change, but now I am able to focus on what I can do to make things better.

Though he avoided going into detail about the turbulence between his parents, Winchester mentioned that their rocky relationship was hard on him as a kid with younger siblings. He was raised Christian, and, as you can see here, he remains devout. So does his wife. In our interview, Winchester, like others, said that church gave him stability and a strong network. He also said that the other main reason he returned to church is because church provides certain values for raising his children. He wants them to also have a moral compass.

What I find to be most interesting is that Winchester implies that believing in a higher power allows him, to an extent, to *surrender* some of his own agency and power. But this "giving up control" is quite therapeutic. Sometimes that kind of surrender is just the respite that someone who has experienced many struggles needs. Functionally, having faith allows him to focus on other important things instead of what he cannot control. According to Winchester, going to services took away his deeply rooted anger in a way that other environments could not. He surrendered his emotional handicap through his belief in a higher power.

Some literature on grit contends that the more control individuals feel over their life and their desired outcomes, the more likely it will be that they achieve more goals. This self-assurance then further increases a person's desire to work harder toward *more* future goals through a sort-of reinforcement process (Duckworth et al., 2007; Kwon, 2017). At the same time, some of this scholarship suggests that overbelieving in factors such as fate, luck, or a higher power can keep individuals from exerting effort toward goals (Hitlin & Kwon, 2016).

Alternatively, I now believe that this type of freeing oneself up mentally that Winchester describes is closely related to purpose and is also conducive to obtaining goals. Faith and its associated confidence can allow individuals to clearly see the consequences of their actions and rationalize productive behavior based on a set of standards. Having purpose helps individuals put in the day-to-day effort that grit requires for someone to achieve longer-term goals. Faith (not just the religious kind) is not only conducive to purpose but also can contribute to longer-term agency by allowing people to feel optimistic about their roles and outcomes in life.

For many people, a second component to purpose, beyond being self-less, is improving oneself by taking on new challenges. Angela Duckworth claims that interest is one source of passion, and I am chiming in: People find out what they are interested in by testing their limits through new pursuits. This allows people to find exactly what things they have a particular knack for.

During their childhoods, most of my participants did not have access to many structured activities outside of school. Meanwhile, their more privileged peers were able and encouraged to regularly engage in things like music lessons, art classes, or intramural sports. Today, now that they have slowly and actively built up their own resources and the opportunities available to them, my participants express their appreciation for learning new things. Many mentioned that discovering and pursuing new talents is one of the most rewarding things they can think of. This might seem to go against grit—which often necessitates having an intense fixation on one thing, but I have found that we get to that level of obsession when we home in on what we excel at and want to keep doing.

From my participants, I learned that skills and talents are discoverable when pushing beyond one's comfort zone, out of the realm of mental ease. Six people I spoke with mentioned their ceaseless desire to try new things that lay out of their comfort zone, and four others used the word "stagnation" in describing something they wish to avoid in life. It seems that the trials and tribulations associated with growing up poor strengthened not only their resilience but also their affinity for difficult things.

"Brian" led the direction of our conversation toward comfort zones. He told me that being uncomfortable is normal and that feeling uncomfortable helps him to learn. I asked him for a specific story about this feeling and how it helps him, and he explained:

> So ironically, I am extroverted, but I am the least extroverted of extroverts. I'm kind of an introvert. When somebody asks me to speak in public I sometimes shake onstage when I'm not prepared. I've had to serve as a spokesperson for different events here at the community college. I still do it though. That's where I get uncomfortable, but then I learn. I learn the strategies on how to speak well, speak clearly, speak publicly, and utilize the power of pause, for example.

Brian was one of the most proactive participants in my study; he actively emailed me and followed up regarding his enthusiasm to participate in my research, more than others did. He did not seem to be an introvert at all. At the same time, though, I can very much relate to what he says. I have always been an introverted extrovert, especially since growing up as a shy Brown kid in a predominantly White community.[1] (I include a little on my upbringing and reasons for eventually going into a life of research in the Appendix, where I describe my methods in a little more depth.)

Brian learned to be a little more "extroverted" by putting himself out there, such as through public speaking, even when it was very uncomfortable. As someone who has recently been doing a lot of public speaking, I can attest to the fact that it never really ceases to be challenging. Brian, an immigrant who speaks English with a noticeable accent, may have struggled initially to get in front of larger groups. However, given his enthusiasm for new pursuits, I am certain he continues to improve. After immigrating to New York and completing his associate's degree, Brian got his bachelor's degree on a scholarship from a top-10 college. He is currently spending his summer at Harvard Business School exercising his creativity and learning about the case study method of doing research.

JLo also told me that he continues to improve his skills in different arenas of life by taking on more roles. In other words, he constantly puts himself in situations where he has to learn to navigate new and different responsibilities. His current status as a father, student, and former car dispatcher turned academic advisor represents this well. He elaborates:

In life—in my life anyway—I have to wear so many hats. When I get up in the morning, I have to be a father, I have to be a husband. Then when I get on the train, I have to be a commuter. Then when I get here, I have to be a student, a mentor, and a mentee. Then when I go to my job, I got to be a dispatcher. I have to be nasty sometimes. I have to be authoritative. Then when I go home, I'm a student again because I have to study. Juggling. It's like I said, asking people who have gone through it how they did it. Or ask someone who's never gone through what you are exactly going through, but ask them about their unique challenges. Then apply that to your situation.

JLo's point about wearing multiple hats is very relevant to ideas in sociology, specifically around self-improvement. In his landmark 1934 book, *Mind, Self, and Society*, George Herbert Mead says that in the self-centric human perspective we all embody, the way to really see oneself objectively is through different roles. Related to this, JLo has had an *ever-evolving* view of himself through the different "hats" he wears. JLo is also using circle-jumping, leveraging the help and advice of others in his different networks. When he was a dispatcher before going for his associate's, JLo did not necessarily realize his potential as a college student.

Mead says that through this type of role-playing, the self remains active and creative. This is why children benefit from playing and using their imagination while also learning how to socialize properly as they develop. JLo even appreciates learning the perspective of other people to consider what he would do in their shoes, given what distinct challenges they may be encountering. And JLo continues to excel in different spaces: Soon after our interview, and since graduating from an elite college with his bachelor's, JLo has led a community-based organization aimed at helping new, young fathers locate educational and professional resources. And more recently, in the fall of 2019, he became an academic advisor at a college in the Bronx while also working to finish his master's degree in organizational leadership and training to be an adjunct professor on campus.

Alicia also mentioned that feeling comfortable is not useful for self-betterment. She brought this up when I asked her, "What is one of the most important lessons you feel you have learned in life so far?" She said:

> That mistakes are great. Mistakes are beautiful. Because if everything goes the way we want, we don't learn the value of things. Mistakes are beautiful opportunities to grow, learn, and to value and appreciate things. Accepting and loving struggle goes along with that. We should always want to be uncomfortable. Comfort zones lead to the stagnant state of being, but being uncomfortable causes us to grow and evolve.
>
> This is actually something I've learned recently, especially through a lot of social justice work—that every human being is in fact a human being and should be treated as such, regardless of any negative stigmatizing connotations that society has condemned them with. They are absolutely wonderful and capable and brilliant. That is something I'm glad I learned recently. We're not indoctrinated to think everyone is brilliant, but rather that this idea of brilliance is a very exclusive type of thing. Once we have this mindset of everything and everyone is brilliant, then we are able to not exclude people and come together and work for the greater good.

Alicia reminds us that making mistakes is a natural part of life. She encourages us to keep in mind that mistakes should be reframed as growth opportunities. She goes on to say that if we consider mistakes as opportunities to grow, we can realize that everyone *else* also has the potential to improve. Then, by making this realization, we also begin to recognize that everyone can be in a constant state of development.[2] Embodying this openminded perspective is one step to correcting the many deficit perspectives that exist and surround us like air. Believing this as wholeheartedly as Alicia does can help us realize that schools are gardens where each rose is deserving of reaching the sun.

MENTAL HEALTH, WELLNESS, AND FULFILLMENT BENEFIT FROM MONITORING AND SOCIAL SUPPORTS

The topic of mental health came up naturally and frequently in my research, particularly when participants discussed what brings them happiness, optimism, and hope for the future. In psychology, mental health is a foundational subject. Poor mental health can inhibit one's ability to show self-efficacy by negatively impacting one's self-esteem and confidence (Bandura, 1982, 2006; Seligman, 2006). My participants substantiated the idea that poor mental health lowers a person's belief in their own potential. I find that poor mental health harms the agency and grit of individuals who are striving to reach certain academic and professional goals and that positive mental health fosters these traits. Both of these states can be increasingly complicated by the more adverse circumstances a person has experienced since childhood.

Of my participants, 18% explicitly mentioned being clinically diagnosed with depression without specific prompting outside of asking about wellness; 10% mentioned experiencing or being diagnosed with anxiety (some of whom also mentioned depression); 8% mentioned struggling with mental health in general without having done deeper investigation. Another 12% explicitly mentioned dealing with some form of "trauma" in their lives, though I recorded 18% of them as having experienced "violent" or "sexual" trauma based on my notes of their stories. In general, when my participants discussed mental health, I observed that female participants were much more likely to disclose the specific diagnoses they had received or use clinical terms when talking about their conditions. Almost all of my participants described that the upkeep of positive mental health is one of the most important things in life to them, usually bringing up these topics unprovoked.

I also noticed that many of my participants displayed a keen self-awareness of their emotional states. Some of them talked about closely monitoring their happiness or sadness. According to many of them, maintaining positive mental health is a daily task that requires effort, attention, and *intention*. (A warning: The next anecdoate contains mention of sexual abuse.) "Gabby" could be considered one of my more resilient participants; she was molested by her father from the age of 5. Her mother actively ignored the abuse and refused to come to Gabby's defense when Gabby finally spoke up about it years later. These experiences fueled within Gabby a deep distrust for mentor/authority figures, which took her decades of therapy and support to begin to overcome. She described the various tolls that these events have taken on her:

> I don't feel optimistic always. I have my struggles. I have anxiety and PTSD. I still see someone, and I'm about to start group therapy, which I'm super excited about. This past month was rough, though. It's hard not to dwell on and get negative, but those feelings do pass. I'm learning how to work around them.

Gabby has reached a point where she now appreciates opportunities to speak about extremely painful experiences from her past. She explained that learning to open up to others took patience with herself and practice but that it has paid off, which seems clear from her excitement about group therapy. The way Gabby describes getting over "rough" times and not dwelling on negative emotions bears a resemblance to grit and daily effort. The ability to take one's own mental health "temperature," so to speak, seems to be related to some kind of perseverance, knowing that negative feelings can be fleeting, letting them run their course, and persisting in spite of them.

The importance that my participants placed on maintaining positive mental health may be directly related to facing many complex responsibilities and challenges at very early ages. These include but are not limited to taking care of their siblings while parents worked, helping to pay the family's rent by maintaining a part-time job during school, overcoming a drug addiction, and experiencing violent or sexual trauma. As a result of facing several of these situations simultaneously, some participants have come to view happiness as a *dynamic* concept, something that cannot be had or maintained at all times but that is always worth striving for. (Similarly, grit and agency are dynamic concepts because they can manifest in many ways in different settings by different people.)

About one-fifth of my sample said that in order to hold onto happiness, they find and attach happiness to simple, observable outcomes that are relatively within their control. When I asked J-Stud what is important to him and what brings him happiness, he said:

> Good health, family, financial stability, continuing to learn, inspiring someone else. I think it is important to continue to be an example that you can come from some circumstances, but if you continue to strive and put in the work, you'll be successful.

Like J-Stud, Roxanne stated that she roots her happiness in health and other simple outcomes. I asked her, "What things are important to you?" She replied:

> My health is important to me. I'm focused on being my best self in my career and outside of it. Working out, eating better, overall mental health, and being happy is important. You have to be happy with yourself before being happy in any situation with others.

My takeaway here is that my participants expressed reasonable expectations for their happiness. Not a single person in my research explicitly said that financial gain brings them happiness or facilitates positive mental health, though a few, like J-Stud, mentioned the importance of being financially "stable." Most participants described the idea that happiness and wellness are prerequisites to improving one's financial situation. For example, Roxanne repeated the terms "best self" and "personal growth" many times during our interview as she described working to improve her life and, by association, her daughter's life.

I have also learned that certain support systems can help students gain positive mental-health outcomes. For instance, after Rose was battered by her father, she eventually made the decision to leave home. Immediately following her departure, she spent her days sleeping on friends' couches, which she recalled as a significantly depressing period of time. I asked her what helped her start to overcome those feelings. Rose said that those types of feelings lasted a long time, and that they eventually improved after enrolling in community college. She described the effect that one mentor had on her:

> When I started [community college], my mentor in the lab, I eventually told her my story. She's the one who tells me I can't give up and it makes me feel better. "You've come so far." I think sometimes you need a reminder. Sometimes even I forget. I'm 24! I don't think about all that stuff, you know? You can't do it completely alone. Even if it's verbal support from someone saying, "Hey, you're smart, you've got this!" I didn't realize that before. Because if you'd talked to me a couple years ago, I'd have told you, "You need to do it alone. No one's going to help you."

Being able to ask for help has brought Rose happiness, whereas being unable to seek help was a handicap for her before. I often tell her story to educators to make the point that sometimes our students who have faced the toughest challenges are harder to reach because they think they have to always go it alone. Yet these are the students who stand to benefit the most when we make ourselves available to them.

Like many students from tough backgrounds, Rose believed that individuals have to work hard by themselves to achieve goals. Her mentor showed her what most who have achieved some success already know: Receiving help from others is not only important but necessary. Rose was able to start opening up to the mentor only slowly over time, over their common interest in biology in the science lab.[3] The mentor listened as she heard Rose's story unfold while constantly offering her encouragement. As I explained in the previous chapter, when a mentor takes a mentee's circumstances into consideration and is respectful of that mentee's identity as well, the mentee is much more likely to feel cared for and to flourish.

Again, the varied, difficult experiences endured by the people portrayed in this book had a significant influence on their perspectives on life. Stan connects optimism to a feeling of contentedness, of being happy and grateful for what he already has. Stan, like every other participant of this research, grew up quite poor. But Stan also lacked stability, moving in and out of shelters with his mother, who suffered from mental illness and could not hold a job. Having reflected on those experiences, Stan mentioned that one of his biggest life lessons has been the importance of gratitude:

> One of the major life lessons that I've learned is to be happy with what you have. Things could be a lot worse. I'm surrounded by people who complain about daily life and struggles, and I think, "Hey, you don't know what I'm going through or have gone through, or compared to other people who are really struggling." Find some way to be happy no matter what's going on. If you're miserable, you're stagnant. And then you can't see the light at the end of the tunnel.

Stan uses the word "stagnant," as did Alicia when she described mistakes as being beautiful. Stan also mentioned being a person who looks for opportunities to grow and who learns from mistakes. Most of my participants do not see the failures they have experienced as inherently bad; this belief is related to understanding what they have already overcome and endured, and what it took for them to do so. I find that poor mental health does not necessarily result simply from failing in one's pursuits but rather is more frequently present when someone lacks the support system they desperately need as they struggle along the way.

While some people might believe that being content is somehow also being unmotivated to strive, I have come to see it as quite the opposite: Contentedness and gratitude can fuel one's motivation to achieve greater feats, which in turn bring additional, reinforcing satisfaction. Being optimistic is a key component to someone maintaining the drive to succeed (Seligman, 2002, 2006).

UNDERSTANDING BURNOUT FROM A SOCIAL PERSPECTIVE

Most people know that constantly striving to reach certain goals through tremendous hard work can take various tolls. So my participants' stories are not simply about triumphing over challenges and finding eventual happiness. Rather, these are narratives about continuing to improve, persevering over difficulties, and developing grit and agency over the course of one's life. They are also largely about the stamina needed to continuously improve and be engaged in the face of sometimes-Herculean tasks. These are some of the most basic realities of the human experience and the quest to keep evolving.

One of my most eye-opening findings has been learning about what my participants referred to as "burnout"—a feeling of exhaustion from incessantly trying to achieve and climb the social ladder. I have decided to make this section more in-depth than others by providing background information, as well as my own independent research, which has been organized in a format that can be useful in real-world contexts. Realizing the commonness of burnout is incredibly important if we want to better understand college persistence, especially for minority students who struggle to stay in college more than White students do (Fruchter et al., 2012). This can be especially true for "nontraditional" student populations, such as first-generation college students, who, according to 2019 research, make up 56% of college goers in the United States (RTI International, 2019). College retainment remains an issue for people in these groups; only 27% of first-generation college goers complete bachelor's degrees in 4 years (DeAngelo et al., 2011).

Fifteen of my participants, or close to one-third of my sample, mentioned feeling burnt out or becoming severely disengaged from their goals at some point. I was able to identify these cases by using the most commonly operationalized definition for burnout based on the Maslach Burnout Inventory (MBI), which has been the leading tool to assess burnout for over 30 years. To classify my participants, I adopted the clinical definition of "burnout" commonly used in academic medicine: A syndrome "characterized by emotional exhaustion, feelings of cynicism and detachment (depersonalization), and a low sense of personal accomplishment" (Dyrbye et al., 2014, p. 443; Maslach, Jackson, Leiter, Schaufeli & Schwab, 1986).

Though this kind of burnout has been commonly studied in groups of various professions, typically in human health services (including nurses, health aides, social workers, physicians, counselors, and therapists), it has been used less frequently in broad educational contexts. Furthermore, burnout has been most common in psychological studies but is relatively absent in sociological scholarship, particularly in qualitative-based methods, such as those that inform this book (Jacobs & Dodd, 2003). And while burnout has been studied in some educational research—it is most prominent in studies about teacher burnout—this phenomenon has been less prevalently observed in students (Embich, 2001; Farber, 1991).

First, it is important to understand that burnout is a mental health issue. According to the Centers for Disease Control and Prevention (2018), mental health includes one's "emotional, psychological, and social well-being." I find that getting burned out can diminish people's feelings of self-worth as well as their confidence. Camila, who considered dropping out in her first year of college, elaborates:

This is corny, but my happiness and health are most important—and family. Not so much school anymore. In high school, I did so much. I would wake up at 6:00 A.M., go to school, go to work, and do programs. I would get home at 7:00 or 8:00 P.M. every day and then I had homework. I was always overwhelmed. I was accepted to my number-one college, but the summer entering freshman year I didn't want to go. I was just . . . I felt burnt out. I couldn't tell my mom that I wanted to take a year off. My sister didn't do that, so that would have been unheard of for me, the star student.

Camila mentions that her happiness and health are most important to her today; however, it was the effect of certain difficulties that led her to develop this perspective. She says that school used to be high on her list of priorities; she graduated as salutatorian (second-highest rank) of her class, but when it came time to start college, she found herself falling into academic burnout. She ended up taking a semester off and regaining her motivation.

Succeeding in college requires that a student integrate both academically and socially on campus (Hartley, 2011; Tinto, 1987). For some students—again, those who have not had experiences that easily translate to college life—the process can be much harder than it seems. Students like Camila, who have had multiple taxing responsibilities at home and work, deal with all of that on top of their academics. Sometimes the culmination of many responsibilities makes burnout imminent, and in light of everything else, academic tasks can easily fall to the wayside.

The Seriousness of Burnout and "John Henryism" for College-Going Strivers

In my 2019 research on college student burnout, I explain that racial minority *strivers*, or those who have been heavily college and career inclined since childhood (Kim, Sax, Lee, & Hagedorn, 2010), may experience a phenomenon now being referred to as "John Henryism," wherein they overburden themselves, through increased grit and resilience, in competitive academic contexts (Kundu, 2019; McGee & Stovall, 2015). These are the same students included in this book; they have had very high expectations to go to college from an early age, which were either self-imposed or imposed by others close to them. In demonstrating high levels of grit for most of their life, despite constantly navigating structural disadvantages, they may have overburdened themselves to the point that they no longer felt a deep connection to long-term goals. The scholars who evaluate grit and its merits have seldom considered that there might be unintended consequences of grit—or pinpointed dedication over long-term periods.

So far I have worked to build up a case that these strivers of color from low-income backgrounds likely feel additional pressures to break the cycle of intergenerational poverty that they have experienced. I have given examples showing that by climbing the social ladder, these people want to improve conditions for their families and communities. The term "John Henryism" refers to an African American folktale in which John Henry wins a race to build a railroad against a steam-powered hammer, but he dies from the resulting stress on his heart. Though this is an incredibly depressing metaphor to apply to our underrepresented, college-bound students, I would like you to now consider that there is at least a reasonable analogy here.

Some research shows that while strivers display grit and behaviors that lead to stable careers, sometimes their resilience may be only "skin deep."

In fact, below the surface, there might be latent health complications, even to the extent that these students experience a faster cellular aging rate than their peers (Brody, Yu, Chen, Beach & Miller, 2016). Our students who work themselves so hard to have a shot at the American Dream might actually be aging themselves faster than others who have always been better supported.

Over time, though they may be presenting an outward appearance of strong academic performance, students can develop severe psychological and physical conditions, including anxiety, depression, suicidal ideation, diabetes, and even heart disease (Brody et al., 2016; James, 1994; McGee & Stovall, 2015). "Princess" told me about her first, overt bout with anxiety, which happened when her academic responsibilities started to build up:

> I had an anxiety attack on the train, which was completely new to me. It was the first time it'd ever happened. I think that I was doing too much again. My first semester, I took five classes, and I didn't know that was allowed. Then, the second semester I said, "Let me take four classes," but they were intense. I did extracurricular activities, and because I was doing so well, I got more responsibilities. I was fulfilling other people's expectations so much that one day, I had an exam, I had to present a research paper, and I was coordinating an event all in one day. The 10 minutes right before my class started, I was on the train about to get off, and I was crying. I couldn't breathe. That scared me. I was falling off the wagon mentally. It was a whole different kind of situation I encountered. I cope better with my anxiety now, but I still struggle with anxiety occasionally.

Not wanting to appear undeserving compared to her classmates, Princess assumed more and more responsibilities. Eventually the weight of these responsibilities was too much to bear, resulting in an anxiety attack. This attack luckily helped Princess come to terms with taking necessary precautions, such as enrolling in student mental health services to cope.

Bright and once highly motivated students (like Princess and Camila) often find themselves, for the first time, feeling isolated and helpless in college environments. Academic priorities can easily slip away as students struggle to reconcile their cultural identities against newly developing college student identities. During the juggling act, it can become difficult to fully notice one's mental struggles, especially if someone cannot count on support from the people around them.

In general, college students are almost expected to be resilient and demonstrate grit as they navigate a new environment while having multiple responsibilities and activities (coursework, relationships, extracurricular activities, healthy habits, partying, and even social media). But it's easy to forget, even for those of us teaching courses, that a subset of them also regularly experience institutional and racial barriers in society and on campus (Kundu, 2019; McGee & Stovall, 2015).

During my college years, I felt protected by our University of Chicago Police Department (UCPD), which boasted being one of the largest private police forces in the world, right after that of the Vatican (Gold, 2014). I also remember that many times, depending on the appearance of the group I was with, I could roam relatively freely on campus with an alcoholic beverage in hand. On the flip side, my Black classmates often mentioned being stopped by officers on patrol and being questioned about whether they actually went to school with us. Those of us who care about equity in higher education cannot overlook the importance of having a truly welcoming college environment and culture, one which is not guided by inherent bias or prejudice.

There is a dire need for new research that looks more thoroughly at the important connection between mental health and wellness and achievement. As education researchers, we should examine how a student's outcomes (e.g., the ability to graduate on time) are the products of a myriad of factors that go well beyond the student's individual-level characteristics. I personally believe that we should also focus on social and institutional resources to help underrepresented students show off their strength of character traits in college settings (Kundu, 2017). Doing so might make research more productive: While it is important to acknowledge the existence of certain recurring problems, it is equally important to offer tangible, tailored solutions based on what we have learned.

Thus, regarding burnout, from here I will: (a) illuminate characteristics that can lead college students to burnout via isolation, and (b) provide an account of the subsequent factors that may help people reconnect with their college pursuits.

Losing Sight of Purpose:
Overly Independent Attitudes and Fulfilling Others' Expectations

The participants who experienced burnout mentioned developing the mentality that no burden was too heavy for them to handle. Over time, they allowed themselves to believe that they could succeed without help, an idea illustrated in this quote from "Nadira":

> I had acclimated to doing things of my own accord instead of looking for help. That has been my downfall, because I need help. That's what my therapist has told me.

Nadira grew up in Bedford-Stuyvesant, Brooklyn, which she told me was a tough neighborhood. During our interview, she did not speak highly of her father, who she said had a lifelong struggle with alcohol abuse. Even though her friends were less academically inclined than she was, Nadira cared about maintaining her good grades. She went to a community college to pursue her associate's degree in liberal arts and joined the honors program, which helped her get into an elite college in Manhattan for her bachelor's degree. Yet during her junior year in college, she experienced tremendous burnout and was unable to perform academically or to even physically show up to class.

When students of color from low-income backgrounds try to deal with their struggles alone, they may start to lose sight of their original motivations for certain academic pursuits. Camila, elaborating on her feelings of burnout as she was preparing to enter her first year of college, says:

> But I honestly feel like part of me didn't want to be in college. I was dragging my body to do stuff that I knew that I *had* to do, but I didn't really *want* to do. And that was very counterproductive.

Camila's initial burnout experience at the end of high school eventually spilled into her first year of college. Over time, her energy diminished greatly as she sometimes had to "drag" her body to class. This lack of energy and motivation caused her to miss class and assignments for the first time in her life. From tirelessly working so hard for so long, she lost a sense of purpose, forgetting why college even mattered to her at all in the first place. Camila effectively lost sight of the fact that she was attending her top-choice college.

Again, sometimes students who grow up in poverty are most fueled by the desire to appease others. Camila wanted to take a break before college, but in the end she decided not to disappoint her mom, placing her family's expectations above her own ideas of what mattered (Carey, 2016). The story of Camila is similar to the story of Princess (who had an anxiety attack on the train to class) because we see a common sense of hopelessness for these students as they take on too much and are unable to rationalize why they are doing so. Princess mentioned pushing the boundaries of her own resilience, due to her desire to please her mentors and because she associated self-worth with her accomplishments. Though she may or may not have had some anxiety before going to community college, the stressors there led to more. Thankfully, her self-awareness kicked in and helped her realize she was prone to anxious outbursts.

If college students lack a sense of belonging, then their self-confidence can diminish, and experiencing burnout (to the extremes of physical and mental illness) becomes more likely (Jacobs & Dodd, 2003). My participants helped me realize that attempting to cope with intense pressures, along with the counterintuitive strategy of overexerting oneself instead of seeking help, can have gravely adverse health-related effects (Gaydosh, Schorpp, Chen, Miller, & Harris, 2018). While the sense of purpose a person feels toward their goals can be motivated by an overall desire to help others, it is important to understand that purpose can be equally reinforced through the help *of* others. Fostering help-seeking behavior also benefits from help.

GUIDED SELF-REFLECTION CAN HELP A PERSON RE-REALIZE THEIR PASSIONS AND REIGNITE THEIR AGENCY

Students who experience extreme struggles in their lives (homelessness, neglect, abuse, or other traumas) may have a weakened belief in themselves and their own abilities. This lower self-efficacy may lead someone to also lose sight of the long-term values of education, even if they are already in college (Bandura, 1986; Jacobs & Dodd, 2003; McGee & Stovall, 2015). Experiencing disparities and unfavorable cultural or racial climates in college can increase a person's feelings of isolation and diminish their self-confidence even further (Chavous, 2005; Comstock et al., 2008; McCabe, 2016; Quaye & Harper, 2014).

Recent research on the cerebral development of young adults reveals that when students are able to think about their own vision, through mentorship or coaching, their cognitive functions can improve (Boyatzis, Jack, Cesaro, Passarelli, & Khawaja, 2010). Mentoring that is focused on addressing academic and professional goals can lower a person's stress levels, and this is especially true for first-generation college-going students (Boyatzis et al., 2010; Creswell et al., 2005). It's reasonable to think that when college students are helped to reconnect with their purpose and academic goals, they are more able to demonstrate the character traits, like grit, that allowed them to succeed in the first place (Cholewa, Goodman, West-Olatunji, & Amatea, 2014; Kundu, 2018).

I have found that when college students are experiencing burnout or are rapidly losing motivation, mentors and role models can provide immensely beneficial aid through "guided" self-reflection. Positive affirmation from another person can improve confidence, especially when the person providing the support is culturally respectful. Just as underrepresented students can lose sight of purpose by tirelessly working to win the approval of others (Carey, 2016; Kundu, 2019; McGee & Stovall, 2015), they can regain purpose through the support of others (Kundu, 2017, 2019). My participants described and credited forms of what I refer to as "guided self-reflection" as helping them get back on track toward their goals. Guided self-reflection can be provided by a family member or mentor who values a student's interests and goals, or even by someone at the institution, such as a college counselor who is an expert on mental health (Quaye & Harper, 2014).

The following quotes highlight this idea:

One of the things that my counselor told me was that it seemed like my self-esteem and my achievements depended on how well I did in school. That kind of hit me. (Princess)

That second half of the year, where I was dismissed from the school—I don't know what led me to finally realize that I needed help. And there were so many people willing to help. Why didn't I do that before? That's something that I definitely embody now. Also *giving* help. It's hard to be here at [this elite college] for a lot of students. It's really emotionally straining for people of all backgrounds, here. I've learned that it's really helpful to be there for each other. Even talking. I've learned to reach out to my advisor a lot of times and let him know what's up, even though he would always be checking anyway. (Liz)

I'm always seeking out mentors, trying to learn something from somebody who is in a senior position, or to get a different perspective, or words of encouragement. Being able to tell my story and have people say, "J-Stud. You know what? It sounds like you've been through a lot, but you've persevered. I like that about you, and I want you to stay in touch and let me know how I could help you." (J-Stud)

These examples of other people acting as positive influences are also representations of cultural competency. Guided self-reflection helped Princess finally realize that her own self-esteem was most tied to academic achievement and pleasing others. Princess told me that realizing this simple fact was incredibly useful in managing her anxiety. Ten of my participants, one-fifth of my sample, mentioned routinely relying on counseling services to improve their mental health and well-being. In nearly every case, they told me this information unprompted, which makes me think that more of them might have mentioned it if I had asked outright. Before I embarked on this project, I did not fully realize the extent to which mental wellness would emerge in my data, and had I anticipated it I would have incorporated related questions into my interviews.

From Liz, we see the important ideas that it is never too late to ask for help and that receiving help is contagious. Liz adeptly highlights that everyone has to rely on others to succeed in college, even though it comes more naturally to some to ask for a helping hand. And, as mentioned in Chapter 4, J-Stud continually seeks out mentors, sometimes simply for positive words of encouragement to stay motivated. This practice was daunting at first, but through repetition, he refined it over time. As one of the few Black men working in investment banking, J-Stud described feeling out of place once in a while. His story is a good example of how mentorship and guided reflection can foster a person's continued help-seeking behavior, even beyond academic settings.

CONCLUSION

In this chapter, I provided an overview of elements that my participants described as necessary for continuing their journey toward economic stability and fulfillment. I learned about how purpose plays an immensely important role in guiding people as they seek self-improvement. For some, the idea of feeling stuck in place can be worse than making mistakes on the road to self-discovery. Many of my participants described this almost constant desire to keep evolving and to avoid stagnation. "Mario" sums up this sense of urgency:

> I got into a street fight once. We lived in an apartment, and we would hear gunshots. My school did not challenge me. With all that, I was growing complacent. It's something that I fear a lot, rooted in the fact that I went to Newark public schools. I fear complacency the most. I don't think I would be at [this private university], honestly. I wouldn't have had challenging classes. I wouldn't have extracurricular activities. I wouldn't have added substance to my life. That's something that is really important to me right now, that my life has substance and that I'm working twice as hard all the time to be the best person I can be.

What surprised me is that this fear of "complacency" was often triggered by my participants' inherent desire to do good. It was also inherently fueled by their need to protect all the hard work they have done over the years. Speaking with them reminded me that the world desperately needs more people who are driven by their concern for others and their desire to serve their communities.

Perspective-driven purpose may be why Tyrique works in the anti-incarceration movement today; why Imperial, who grew up in public housing, desires to go into urban planning to help the Bronx "revitalization" projects be community-minded; why Alicia scoffs at the idea of going to work on Wall Street because her mother is a cafeteria worker; and yet purpose-led perspective is also why J-Stud, who in fact is a Wall Street banker, still lives in Jamaica, Queens, serving as a role model for the kids there. Allowing these seeds to blossom and express their individual tenacity to reach the sun required ample amounts of social support and respect for their personhood.

These individuals each provide an example of Paolo Freire's (1968/1972) praxis, or the concept that a combination of both action and reflection can be used to work against the structures that affect people's lives. Our collective responsibilities to help each child, eventually leading them to a seat at the table, can help us find solutions to problems we have historically been trying to tackle. By helping our most vulnerable students, we can find that they want to return the favor and help more students like themselves.[4]

Hector enjoys volunteering at his former high school, which places his own achievements into perspective:

> I have students come to me from the high school that I went to. I still have relationships with the football coaches there. I'll tell them, "This is all about figuring out what you want to do. This is about figuring out what you enjoy doing. Don't put this immense pressure on yourself where now you have to figure out what's the most lucrative career. I feel that those things are going to work themselves out.
> You are going to make the best decision for you once you are more informed. Right now, you have to ask questions." I stress a lot, "You have to ask questions. You have to be curious. Don't be afraid to ask questions."

Interestingly, you may recall from Chapter 3 that Hector referred to his school and the people there as not "giving a shit," which expedited him dropping out. Yet despite these negative experiences, Hector goes back to help the current students there because he now realizes the significant impact his presence and influence have. This reflective strategizing, which is one of the components to my definition of agency, is what led him to pursue a master's in social work. It has occurred to me that forms of selflessness can be taught or largely fostered by the help of others.

From hearing these stories, I have come to realize that having grit does not mean needing to maintain an *undeterred* focus on one *task* at a time; instead, I now more clearly understand what Duckworth means by saying that grit requires undeterred focus on certain goals over longer-term periods. Liz personifies this apparent conundrum. Even though she described having immense trouble sitting in place and focusing all her attention on one task at a time—which is sometimes necessary to write a college paper—she overcame those challenges, and her burnout, through her grit for going to college.

Liz is one of the participants who had to take a leave of absence because of failure to complete assignments on time and underlying burnout. But her long-term focus was on getting her scholarship back and finishing her college degree. She was fixated on not just going back to any school but to the same elite institution that had placed her on a year-long probation. I asked her why she did not care to transfer to a less rigorous institution, and she said:

> I guess I like to finish what I start—what I always start. So I just *have* to come! It wasn't an option for me to go anywhere else. I had to get *this* degree from this college. I spent time thinking about what I wanted to do. Because what was the point, if I was just going to come here and let the same thing happen again?

Here, Liz epitomizes grit by saying that she has to get through what she puts on her plate. She reminds us that grit does not need to look like one specific type of engagement from a student. Even our students with severe ADHD may have grit, which we can help unlock if we simply are able to notice it. It is also important to note that in her quote, Liz mentions that she realized she needed to take the time to figure out what she wanted to do. Through her support system, she was eventually able to remember why she wanted to attend college in the first place and to regain the motivation to overcome her burnout and graduate only one year behind schedule.

My findings on burnout, thanks to my participants' explicit mentions of the term, challenge the idea that tremendous hard work and grit are *objectively* good. In fact, when students are not supported adequately, they may develop severe mental health issues, such as anxiety or depression, from overwork. Despite the commonness of burnout and these related wellness problems, people often fetishize students of color who are successful, praising their relentless work ethic instead of also addressing that there are systemic factors at play and disparate outcomes along racial lines (Mohammad, 2016). We should be mindful of such tendencies; the prominence of positive psychology in education research has brought about a recent resurgence of ideas related to resilience, such as grit (Ong, Bergeman, & Bisconti, 2004; Seligman & Csikszentmihalyi, 2014). There is a responsibility on our part as a society to destigmatize mental illness and, for our young people, to focus holistic efforts on prevention rather than work on dealing with problems after they've surfaced.

To avoid serious health-related issues such as burnout, students should be guided and encouraged to routinely monitor their wellness. Guided self-reflection, with the help of a therapist or mentor who demonstrates cultural competency (I will provide more examples of what this looks like, in schools specifically, in the next chapter), can help a student like Liz to remember her reasons for chasing certain endeavors. Simply striving to reach a vague concept of self-improvement or to appease others cannot dampen impending burnout. Maintaining focus on purpose is necessary for pursuing long-term goals in the face of huge responsibilities and challenges, as is recognizing that academic achievement and financial success cannot be the only components of living a fulfilled life.

CHAPTER 6

Conclusion

Fighting the Normalization of Failure

On December 3, 2014, a diverse group of thousands marched through busy New York streets, carrying signs and bellowing chants. The night was dark and misty as the marchers' hot breaths haunted the sky. Red flashing lights from police barricades illuminated the path, yet also added to the tense feelings surrounding the scene.

Officials watched intently to make sure that the peace was not disturbed. The protestors marched more than 40 blocks, from 14th Street in Union Square toward Rockefeller Center for the annual lighting of the Christmas Tree. They were not fueled by yuletide cheer but instead by the absence of justice. This was one more explosion from too many dreams deferred.

In July of 2014, Eric Garner, an unarmed Black man, was killed in the New York City borough of Staten Island by a police officer using an illegal chokehold. Though the coroner listed the death as a homicide, a grand jury chose not to indict the officer responsible for the inhumane death. The decision took place just a week after the Ferguson decision, in which a grand jury in Missouri chose not to indict Darren Wilson, the officer who shot and killed unarmed, Black 18-year-old Mike Brown in August of the same year.

Ferguson ignited a type of national fervor unseen in decades. Protests, rallies, sit-ins, and student "die-ins" shut down roads and bridges, schools, and other institutions and public spaces. The Black Lives Matter movement promised to disrupt the quiet harmony of everyday American life. It threatened to continue to expose uncomfortable social hypocrisies if considerable changes were not made. The United States was forced to revisit the honesty of racial profiling and question the reality of whether we truly live in a postracial society.[1]

*

I wrote the preceding words the day after attending the protest.[2] I was sitting in the NYU Bobst Library processing the recent events, trying to understand their effects on me and those around me. At that time, as a second-year graduate student without an office to my name, I wondered if any of the students studying around me with their heads down were also thinking about race politics. Heading home, I felt some reassurance when I saw a poster on campus that asked, "Why, when a Black student is admitted to an elite college with a scholarship is it because of his race, but when he is killed by a cop, it's not?"

That was my first semester teaching the course American Dilemmas, and there seemed to be plenty of dilemmas for us to discuss. I remember asking my students, "What's a 'die-in'?," and learning that hundreds of students would later congregate in the Bobst lobby, lying down on the floor as a sign of protest. They laughed when I naively admitted I thought it meant that students all over campus would just fall down in place wherever they were at that time—I mimicked falling down mid-lecture to join them in solidarity. (I thought maybe the die-in was similar to the "same-time pencil-drop" that elementary school students across the world try to coordinate to disrupt their teachers.)

That actual die-in was moving. Seeing so many students lying there— some of them mine—is an image I cannot forget (see Figure 6.1).

And since that week, in the many years that have followed, there have still been some incredibly tense moments in our lives. On some of them, it has been difficult to *teach*—something that I know resonates with educators in both K–12 and in higher ed who meet their students every day.

Figure 6.1. Student "Die-In"

Photo courtesy of Michael Gould-Wartofsky

For me, one of the hardest days was Wednesday, November 9, 2016, the day after Donald Trump's presidential win. Like many, I was pretty stunned by the outcome and was at a loss for words. The night before, I briefly contemplated canceling class as some others had done, but I realized that was a cop-out. I figured my students, to better learn, deserved an opportunity to first process their feelings on one of the most memorable days in American history. I owed it to them to create a space to decompress and even vent if they needed to, or perhaps to even quietly be cheerful if Trump was the person whom they wanted to win. Either way, everyone deserved the opportunity to get together. I sent out a midnight email saying that class would still be on at 9:30 A.M.

I did cancel whatever scheduled lesson I had planned for that day. There was nearly perfect attendance and we made a circle of desks. I told my students to keep in mind that one in five of their fellow New York City residents had voted for this outcome and that even if they vehemently disagreed (a drastic understatement for many) to remember to be respectful to one another. Then I opened up the floor for them to speak freely. I led a short discussion but mostly chose to learn from them that day.

Our students have to be brought to the table because they will decide our future. This is especially true in times of social unrest and disconnect because, ideally, they will learn how to collaborate and live in harmony from these moments.

I truly believe that if our schools and educational institutions can celebrate individuality by using differences to educate, we will all be better off. The strength of our future democracy depends on it. In 2017, children of color made up the majority population of youth in 14 states. And demographers predict that soon, around 2020, youth of color will represent the majority of U.S. children and that around 2040 there will be no clear racial majority in the nation (Annie E. Casey Foundation & Center for the Study of Social Policy, 2019; Frey, 2018). I often wonder, when that day does come, will we come closer to representing the same *human* race, or will groups become more isolated and disparities worsen?

America's story is characterized by varied privileges, as well as the willingness by some and unwillingness by others to acknowledge them. These privileges, or lack thereof, are not always related to race, either; on the contrary, poor White citizens are often relegated to second-class status. And if we are unable to acknowledge these realities, it seems unfair to then go about pretending that this nation is living up to its intended potential of justice for all.

SHIFTING PARADIGMS ABOUT WHAT'S POSSIBLE

My purpose has been to offer suggestions for how to build the capacity of young people, specifically focusing on how to foster their grit and agency. I use education as the landscape for investigating how schools and pedagogy can foster the abilities of our students. Schools should not have to bear the burden of fixing social problems that come from beyond their walls but very much impact what happens inside them—unequal teacher pay, lack of teaching supplies, potential lead poisoning affecting a child's brain development. However, they are the best-suited institutions for unlocking the latent potential of our citizens. As a nation, we need to identify and implement solutions to better support schools so that they can, in turn, better support our students.

Each individual I included in this book is remarkable, and each has a uniquely complex story. I hope that by organizing and compiling their narratives, I was able to give you a sense of the factors that can help students strive toward academic and professional goals despite challenges. Yet I am certain that questions remain about how to connect and incorporate my research and theories into practice to help students tap into their agency and channel their grit. To be fair, that was my motivation for putting my findings on paper.

For a school that is strapped for resources, or for a novice teacher trying to connect with seemingly disengaged students, what parts of this are directly *actionable*? Is it realistic for all teachers to recognize that a student's talent for creating rap lyrics can eventually translate into literacy, leading to a path for college and a stable career? My students, many of whom are bright-eyed and eager to enter urban classroom settings and lend their services to the community, often ask these and even harder-hitting questions. In classes like my American Dilemmas course, we speak about many of the limits of public education.

But we also speak about the *possibilities*. I lead my students back to the question that frames my book. Instead of wondering about all of the reasons why students with fewer resources can fail, why don't we look at the many ways in which they can learn to thrive? How can we best reach them even if our capacities are limited? And, because seeing is believing, I take my students to visit two schools that run on a philosophy of high expectations and support for each student. These are schools with infectious energy where staff and students take great pride in their shared accomplishments. More importantly, these are the schools with a population of students who might have felt marginalized or disenfranchised had they attended school elsewhere.

Educating Through the Visions of Medgar Evers and James Baldwin

We are headed to Crown Heights in Brooklyn, then to Chelsea in Manhattan. We are visiting Medgar Evers College Prep and the James Baldwin School, respectively. Walk into either one, and you are immediately greeted by a loud, vibrant atmosphere that makes your head tilt back an inch like air-conditioning does when you step inside from a humid summer day. Welcome to the frenzied poetry in motion of high school.

The students see that you have entered *their* space. They might give you a funny but soft look, perhaps making an aside to their friends that you do not quite catch. Evers students are wearing simple red or yellow polo shirts and slacks as a uniform. Administrators are very present, warmly scolding them to walk in an orderly and tame fashion. At Baldwin, there are no uniforms, and there is less order in general. It is boisterous. Students are unlikely to be reprimanded for having their phones out.

At both schools, you will also notice that colorful student work takes over the hallways. At Evers, you are likely to see hundreds of student spotlights and college announcements for where students are declaring they will go next. You may also see these sprinkled throughout Baldwin, but you may be more intrigued to stop and learn about influential people of color, from either history or the present day, that these students look up to.

Now we should mention some basic facts. Both schools receive federal Title 1 funding; all students qualify for free or reduced-cost school meals. Close to 100% of the students are racial minorities. Medgar Evers has higher than a 90% graduation rate, and most of their students go to college on scholarship. At Baldwin, which is a partner of New York City's Outward Bound Schools[3] network, students graduate on a rolling basis during different times of the year. About half of Baldwin students are over the New York City Department of Education (NYCDOE) age range for secondary school. They have transferred to Baldwin for a second chance at getting their high school diplomas.

But more is going on than meets the eye. The kind of central and unifying cultures that exist at these schools, trickling down from the leadership, to staff, to students, do not just form overnight. They are not easy to create. In the secret sauce is both the acknowledgment of all the barriers to forming academic identities that we have discussed and an unwavering vision to not let any of that be an excuse that blocks the way of these kids.

Creating Bridges to Educational Expectations

As we have discussed, sometimes students have a hard time reconciling what they see as their cultural identity with the identities needed and expected of them to succeed in school (Noguera, 2009; Ogbu, 1992; Ransaw & Majors, 2016). But students from all backgrounds generally do believe in the idea that education is a pathway for success in life—even if they don't necessarily believe it applies to them specifically (Carter, 2003; Mickelson, 1990). Unfortunately, despite believing that education helps *some* people, students are likelier to achieve based on what they see happening closest to them: Did my parents graduate and think about school fondly? Are my peers thriving in school, or are they dropping out? We cannot blame the students who are simply being attentive to the disparities they notice around them.

Countering these festering forces requires a fundamental belief in all students' potential. It requires believing that students would be ready to

Figure 6.2. Principal Michael Wiltshire of Medgar Evers College Prep at the Head of the Class

Photo courtesy of Michael Wiltshire

put in the effort they need to achieve if we could just meet them where they are. We have thoroughly discussed concepts in psychology and how the grit a student shows, or the mindset they display for academics, is not just *inherited* but is also largely a function of their environment, moldable under the right conditions (Duckworth, 2016; Dweck, 2008). Evers and Baldwin begin with the message that thinking "not those kids" is an unacceptable cop-out. The staff remains bold and unified by not only ceaselessly setting high expectations but also creating pathways for students to step up to the challenge. They build on the idea that all students believe in the idea of education, using that as a foundation.

The Evers and Baldwin schools are named after two iconic Black civil rights leaders and freedom fighters. The principals and teachers frequently remind their students of their school's namesake, instilling in them the charge to carry on their legacies. The students are told that they hold the power and duty to uphold the civic responsibilities that come from being an educated citizen. They do community service throughout the city and also proudly let visitors know—as they have told my students and me—what it was that Medgar Evers and James Baldwin contributed to America.

Academic success follows suit. A middle school feeds into Evers College Prep, and middle-schoolers and freshmen enter mandatory summer school with an option to receive weekend tutoring. Many students end up passing multiple New York State Regents Exams by 9th grade. And by sophomore year, Evers students are encouraged to take AP courses, of which there are 21 offered. They can take up to 11 college-level credits each semester by their junior year. Not surprisingly, many students end up graduating high school with their associate's degrees in hand. And, in addition to sending some of these scholars to the Ivy League, Medgar Evers is proud to send grads to Historically Black Colleges (HBCs).

For transfer students at James Baldwin, traditional high school might not have been the right fit the first time around. As such, the classes at Baldwin reflect not only what students want to take but also what teachers want to *teach*. Outside of standard core curricula, these courses include, but are not limited to, Islamic Art and Mathematics, the Origin of Racial Slavery, and, of course, Dracula and Gender Identity. In the summer of 2016, I was lucky enough to sit in on a summer class structured completely around Ta-Nehisi Coates's book *Between the World and Me*. With the vast underrepresentation of minorities in educational materials (remember Seku's story from Chapter 4), these integrative approaches allow students to see themselves in what they learn and then to develop academic identities (Horning, Lindgren, & Schliesman, 2014).

Figure 6.3. Principal Brady Smith of the James Baldwin School Celebrating his Students' Accomplishments

Photo courtesy of Brady Smith

The Baldwin School also petitioned for and was granted an official waiver from the New York State Regents Exams. Alternatively, Baldwin students prepare for comprehensive assessments in each subject area. Student essays are reviewed through an academic review process with outside readers from faculty all over the school, as well as through oral defenses, which students present colloquium-style. Students must revise and resubmit if they do not demonstrate competency, though there is ample support for each go-round. They are also given autonomy to choose topics they are interested in because teachers realize these curiosities can give way to genuine lifelong passions.

At both schools, students are constantly given the opportunity to understand how education is relevant to *their* lives, not someone else's.

Consistent Role Models Who Are Consistently Present

When students can relate to their mentors on a personal level, they can better visualize how success could look in their own lives.[4] Giving them access to successful people from similar backgrounds is incredibly powerful. Both Evers and Baldwin actively recruit expert volunteers from the community to help with programming. For example, Evers has a magazine publishing class in which students write, edit, and publish their own editorials, illustrated with compelling art and photos, with partners at the neighboring Medgar Evers College.

Still, the most important role models are those who run these buildings. Teachers at both schools are impressively diverse. Students from minoritized backgrounds have been shown to actually prefer minority teachers, who might be more attentive to the various cultural needs students have or the challenges they face (Cherng & Halpin, 2016). These schools treat faculty diversity like an asset. But, at the same time, the power of genuine relationships transcends race. James Baldwin's principal is Brady Smith, a White male. A former student of his told me:

> He's the best principal anybody could have—the type where he'd be in the main hallway, everybody coming in, and he'd be there. *Everybody's* name, this man knew. "You're supposed to be in the 8:30 class, you'd better get there!" He knew everyone's schedule in his head. Students take note and hold onto these memories, beyond graduation.

These are memories that students cherish their whole lives. I often mention Smith when I speak to groups of educators who wonder if their schools' faculty makeup should resemble their students in terms of race or ethnicity, to better reach the kids. Personally, I tell them, I don't *necessarily* think so. Lacking teachers of color is a clear structural issue, one that needs system-level strategies to fix. But in the end, to reach kids, adults simply need to care about them. Then they can set a tone that high achievement is not just a possibility but an expectation.

Again, it takes persistence for a school to be able to express a unified value system like Evers. Once a failing school, Evers took more than 10 years to turn around. However, through undeterred leadership, an academic culture began to form and has endured the test of time. Early on, principal Dr. Michael Wiltshire clearly expressed to his staff his vision for making the school more immersive. His desire for more involvement meant that Evers would soon offer more programming that extended hours into the day and even into some weekends. Those who embraced the radical change in direction remained at the school, leaving a truly unified teaching force. Figures 6.2 and 6.3 show Principals Wiltshire and Smith, respectively, connecting with their students.

The beneficiaries of the long turnaround process are the students at Evers and Baldwin, who identify as scholars because they are able to take ownership of their education. Through cultural and social supports, they are taught to think critically about the world they inhabit. They can then better understand their potential for creating change within it. In essence, they learn to believe in themselves in the same way that the adults in their schools do. Knowing that these schools care for both their academic and nonacademic needs, some students commute more than 90 minutes each way to attend. The teachers, administrators, advisors, and counselors are ready to greet them by name each morning as they walk in.

We can think of these schools as examples worth following. They are testaments to the kinds of improvements in education that can sometimes require taking a long and arduous road. But sometimes innovation can be as simple as having the audacity to implement common sense. Believing in our students is believing in ourselves. We can put students on a path toward success when we take their backgrounds into consideration, with thoughtfulness toward the many personal and structural barriers the students may face. Similarly, instead of taking the easy way out—such as simply shutting down failing schools and pushing out failed students—we scholars should collaborate with school leaders and staff, parents and communities, policymakers, and, perhaps most importantly, students themselves.

RECOMMENDATIONS FOR FOSTERING GRIT AND AGENCY

The research supporting this book serves two ends: Primarily, we must continue to notice the diverse strengths that students already have as tools to further motivate them. I have challenged often-implicit deficit notions that exist in education about what students are capable of, by instead showing the greater benefits of asset-based approaches. Through my examples in and out of schools, I hope you feel closer to fully believing that success *could* be possible for *any* student—from the teen who unexpectedly becomes a parent to the young man charged with armed robbery—if they are provided with support systems and opportunities that respect who they are. Furthermore, we should broaden our perspective to consider that anyone can be a student worthy of learning and deserving of better circumstances; we should all aspire to be lifelong learners.

The second objective of my research is to provide you with a sense of possibility for helping more students thrive. Earlier I referred to my participants as "exceptional," but I did not mean "exceptions," because they are not simply anomalies. Thinking of them as such only works to massage our concerns about the opportunity gap and absolve us from our responsibilities to do more for students like them. The individuals I introduced in this book are people with real challenges that many of our children encounter. And their success does not mean that our systems are working as much as they highlight that some students can succeed *despite* our systems. We must make our schools more equitable and inclusive. I have shown that there are multiple factors that can facilitate more students' growth toward academic and professional success and that we should work to create similar environments for more students to thrive.

Before I close, I would like to provide a high level, bird's-eye summary of my main takeaways to complement the more focused sections of this book. These are also broken down by the facets of life that we have studied together.

For Homes and Families

Families can foster agency and grit in many ways. The family unit is most effective and strong when it is stable, when children feel nurtured and cared for routinely, even if by a single parent. Some of my participants mentioned that their parents took efforts to shield them from the effects of poverty, making them feel comfortable and safe at all times. Though this was tough on the parents, my participants benefited when they were kids by being able to focus better on activities and academics.

Parents and guardians, despite having fewer financial means, can provide immeasurably great supports to their children by exhibiting examples of strong work ethic. The parent who holds down two jobs to put food on the table shows their children what it means to have grit that can later be applied to more professional career tracks. Additionally, family members are useful in stressing the financial and cultural values of education to their children, as well as teaching about the importance of civic virtues and service. I also learned that having children earlier in life may not necessarily inhibit someone's ability to form goals to keep advancing; instead, for many of my participants, it seemed to catalyze their ability to conceptualize what the future should look like and how to better plan for it. I will elaborate on what this means for stakeholders in the next section.

Finally, I found that students with different disadvantages often experience growing up "too fast." Childhood is an incredibly delicate phase, and many participants lamented having lost the privilege of getting to be a child. Their accelerated entry into adulthood sometimes led them to have a difficult time opening up to others or trusting people who could be vital to them. These individuals have to work quite hard to find adults and mentors with whom they feel comfortable enough to open up. Instead, their default decision might be to burn themselves out to avoid the risk of seeming like a burden to someone else.

I cannot overstate how necessary it is for our youth to have access to mentors who listen to them and safe environments in which to learn and play. For students who grow up in low-income homes, there should be community-based organizations, programs, and services that can lend a helping hand. These important influences allow young people to learn how to trust others as they continue to develop and navigate multiple relationships in their lives.

For School Settings and Institutions of Higher Education

I have provided examples of the different ways that culturally competent mentors and culturally relevant curricula can look. These supports can actually be quite simple, but they help students see themselves in a new light, allowing them to visualize themselves in a variety of new environments with new roles. Through my participants' stories I demonstrated how mentors and networks can help students develop the help-seeking behaviors they will need to reach different goals with the support of others.

Whenever possible, mentors from the community should be invited to offer services and share their experiences with local students. When these individuals share their stories, and possibly even take the time to provide some skill-based training to students, students' worldviews expand. They can also learn the cultural norms that are necessary for thriving in diverse academic and professional settings.

When curricula are more inclusive, emphasizing cultural and ethnic history, students of color may be more likely to make modern connections to their lives through critical thinking. Schools should expand their coverage of diverse and important historical figures, highlighting their impacts on social change and on civil rights. This helps students from diverse backgrounds form racial pride and engage more deeply with academic material. Students can then dream to make similarly important contributions to their community.

I want to stress the incredibly positive benefits that come from academic programming that allows students to experiment productively; this programming might include courses in creative writing, music production, or industrial arts, where students can learn useful but fun skills. Often students from low-income homes, who attend lower-resourced schools, do not have the ability to try their hand at things that more advantaged students might take for granted. Sadly, this can keep some from pursuing what they are interested in, which for many students also means that they do not have the opportunity to find purpose. This is why urban schools desperately need community partners to collaborate with in order to expand the services they can offer.

It can also be beneficial for students to receive soft guidance about normalized cultural expectations that others take knowing about for granted. One example I have seen in different schools is teaching students proper email etiquette. Sometimes, such additional curriculum can be built into advisory classes in which there is more flexibility with content. Giving students seemingly simple information empowers them and will reap enormous rewards for years into the future, as digital etiquette is now a requirement for many entry-level jobs. These cultural tools are necessary for students to successfully navigate social norms and gain entry and climb into different social circles.

Finally, students who grow up with various challenges in unstable environments need spaces to vent and cope safely. All schools should have effective counseling services and mental health resources staffed by highly trained professionals experienced in dealing with situations such as trauma; at a policy level this is a public health issue that should be built into the budget of public schools everywhere. Sometimes kids just need room to be kids and express themselves and their frustrations, and we have to remember that in our educational spaces.

Additionally, students who are parents stand to benefit immensely from easily accessible child care and parenting education services in their schools or in their communities. These services are critical to students' ability to maintain focus on their academic pursuits. The NYC Department of Education offers the Living for the Young Family Through Education, or LYFE program, which provides in-school child care for parent–students in 35 different locations. Services such as LYFE could serve as an opportunity to dampen the social stigma associated with young parenthood so that these students are not counted out from social mobility.

Fostering Agency in Classrooms. I would like to leave my readers who are educators with some simple guidance on how to cater their lessons around fostering agency. Though Chapter 2 included a larger theoretical foundation of agency, I believe that agency can be distilled into simpler parts. Primarily, agency has the same essential components that Paolo Freire describes as making up "praxis," namely action and reflection (Freire, 1968/1972; Nagaoka et al., 2015). Action and reflection inform and influence each other through balance, akin to a yin-yang symbol (see Figure 6.4). Each has their own subcomponents as well.

Figure 6.4. Agency Is Reinforced Through a Feedback Loop Between Action and Reflection

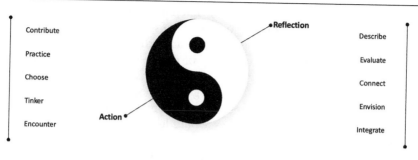

Contribute

Practice

Choose

Tinker

Encounter

Action

Reflection

Describe

Evaluate

Connect

Envision

Integrate

Adapted from University of Chicago Consortium on Chicago School Research, 2015.

Allowing students to play an active and potentially leading role in their own learning is important in ensuring that they continue to develop a sense of autonomy. To encourage agency-building, teachers should work to ensure that at every step a student can answer these questions:

- What exactly am I trying to learn here and why?
- What are the different ways I can show that I have learned or mastered this?
- What is the next thing I should then be able to conquer?
- And if I get stuck, how can I locate the resources I need for help?

Essentially, these are the questions that guide us in everyday life. An educator's righteous goal is to prepare their students for the real world, where they will be expected to set and meet their own goals. Classrooms can be wonderful microcosms in which they can practice, while teachers celebrate students' small gains and hold them accountable through warm yet demanding approaches (Delpit, 2012). If teachers nurture but do not coddle, and if they are clear about their expectations and the reasons for them, students benefit. This is how we coach our students to successfully adapt to new roles and environments, hard as it may be, as they potentially also realize that comfort is an enemy of progress. Discomfort can be fleeting, especially if a person is aware of their reasons for changing directions and mindful of where they seek to go in the end.

A Word on Inclusive Higher Education. My Chapter 5 findings on student burnout around and in college begs a question: If some students are prone to overburdening themselves to the point of exhaustion, is it their fault for failing to locate support systems, or is it the university's fault for not providing a better system for underrepresented students to find needed resources?

I should concede that the word "fault" is perhaps unnecessarily accusatory, but I think that colleges have a real duty to be more culturally responsive toward the varied needs of different, underrepresented student populations. Failing to provide resources like a support center for minority students or those who are first-generation and from low-income homes is a massive oversight that gets in the way of degree completion for students who find themselves in a foreign environment. I have heard firsthand that some students may not realize they can get free books from the library, or that they may not realize the importance of coming to my office hours to make a connection with me, but they would learn these norms from a cohort of peers or supportive staff who want to help them succeed.

Most importantly, institutions of higher education must advocate for the achievement *and* well-being of their constituents who are investing so much of their time, effort, and financial resources to attend. If there is one thing to be learned from the coronavirus pandemic of 2020 for these institutions, it is that they need to be adaptable enough to support students in various, changing contexts in order to remain of value. Otherwise, the sticker prices are too high to justify. Colleges must not only provide certain resources on campus but also promote the continued use of them off-campus and virtually because counseling services often carry an associated stigma. I often tell colleges that are interested in increasing cultural competency training that their officials would benefit by learning some relational cultural theory (RCT). RCT is a framework now widely applied in counseling fields to help address the many different, and often psychological, effects of discrimination that marginalized students face at school and in society.

With foundations in feminist theory, RCT is responsive to needs by emphasizing the importance of relationships to a person's developmental growth and ability to heal; it recognizes that feeling disconnected from or unwelcome around one's peers can cause great personal harm (Cholewa, Goodman, West-Olatunji, & Amatea, 2014; Comstock et al., 2008; Duffey & Somody, 2011). It is relatively well known, though perhaps not very openly discussed, that the rate of death by suicide[5] among college students has long been a serious mental health problem. Colleges and universities still view mental wellness through the narrow lens of how adaptable students are to campus and to leaving home (Byrd & McKinney, 2012; Hartley, 2011). Instead, colleges should realize that well-being also requires healthy social relationships (with peers, faculty, and advisers) to prevent students from experiencing anxiety, depression, and perhaps eventual burnout.

Sometimes college students may try to reject certain parts of their cultural identities to fit in, but as a result they may end up feeling shame, unworthiness, and a lack of confidence (Cholewa et al., 2014; Comstock et al., 2008). Recall the story I told in the Prologue about my student who truly believed that she might not appear "White enough" to do well at NYU, or the one from Chapter 5 in which I mentioned that my college police force unnecessarily interrogated Black undergrads, asking them if they belong. These little things can take tolls on students that manifest mentally and physically over time. Through RCT, universities can implement interventions that promote healing by fostering a student's self-worth (Cholewa et al., 2014; Comstock et al., 2008).

A focus on healing is key to reigniting the inspiration of students who have experienced burnout because it acknowledges that they are experiencing real ailments brought on by adverse circumstances and environmental conditions. Through RCT approaches, students' identities of race and ethnicity are celebrated, perhaps by hosting fun events and showcases on campus (Cholewa et al., 2014; Duffey & Somody, 2011). These events can help students feel connected and empowered through a sense of belonging. When colleges and universities demonstrate that they are invested in the well-being and achievement of their student diversity and take active efforts to serve populations with unique needs, they leave stronger legacies (Quaye & Harper, 2014).

Expanding the Notion of Pathways Through Sharing Best Practices. Though a 4-year college degree should not be necessary for all students to obtain an eventual family-sustaining income and purposeful career, it is largely implicitly required today. For this reason, we should consider what happens in K–12 as integral to discussions on what matters in higher education, and vice versa. Each pathway builds into or comes from the other. As an academic, I can say that we are also guilty of furthering these isolations by considering them to be different subjects. We have conferences, journals, and job titles based around these distinctions. (If I wish to pursue a career as a professor, I am honestly not sure if I will pursue a position in higher education, or urban education, or sociology of education.) But when we make ourselves think toward a K–16 or even a pre-K–20 approach, we allow ourselves to better conceptualize the meaning of lifelong learning and the goal of creating positive social change that sustains and lifts up our communities. Briefly, let me share two models I have come across that put the idea of pathways into practice.

I recently visited Memphis and learned about their new River City Partnership between Tennessee's largest school district, Shelby County Schools, and the University of Memphis (UM), through which passionate local high school students are selected in cohorts to attend UM to study urban education. These "scholars" are then specifically trained throughout college (through immersive courses in education, local history, and content areas) so they graduate certified and ready to take on the challenges of teaching in their own inner city. The grassroots program also provides scholarships to the students, ensuring that the vision is sustainable and that college debt will not extinguish the passion of these eager new teachers.

I also spent 2018 to 2019 researching a new, expansive workforce development project in the South Bronx. Among other organizations, one nonprofit called HERE to HERE is convening a group of high schools, community colleges, and businesses with the goal of preparing students with the broad range of skills needed to enter college and the labor market. High school students partake in work-based learning programs that teach core skills, like interviewing and email etiquette, to successfully land and thrive in summer employment. Some paid internships are offered through the NYC Department of Youth & Community Development's Summer Youth Employment Program.[6] Additionally, businesses commit to summer internships and multiple-year apprenticeships for these students to receive training and certificates to facilitate careers in tech, finance, or health care.

Schools and school districts are too constrained to take on expansive, innovative, and scalable solutions alone. When they connect with partners from different sectors with the goal of uplifting students through asset-based approaches, we can build toward equitable, generational impacts. College access is not, in and of itself, a successful outcome unless we make sure that when students are *in* college they have the tools to keep progressing. Full success is in ensuring that students stay motivated and on track toward securing a purposeful, family-sustaining career. Students need to know how to leverage resources, find reliable mentors, and establish their networks at every level. While some students have been taught this dance from an early age and perhaps flourish more naturally in college and career, others need a little more guidance so that all students can march to the beat of their own drums while strengthening the overall ensemble.

For the Soul, and the Ever-Evolving Self

My participants said that one of the most important things in life is to have a guiding purpose. For them, purpose is overwhelmingly connected to the idea of helping other people who may be facing similar predicaments to the ones my participants encountered. I found that faith (religious or not) allowed participants to maintain a positive outlook and the optimism to persist despite challenges. They felt more confident when they were able to perceive certain obstacles as necessary to overcome as a part of the "grander" scheme of things.

My participants mentioned that they relish the ability to try new things and discover new interests. Many connected their love of discovery to the lack of similar opportunities in childhood. Discovering new skills and passions often meant pushing themselves beyond their comfort zones, but that was described as a natural price to pay to avoid stagnation in life. Their agency relies heavily on the idea of momentum and desire to simply keep moving forward.

Finally, they also expressed the paramount importance of simply and routinely monitoring their mental health. They closely associated their well-being with happiness. When they had neglected their mental health, they were more prone to burnout. I found that burnout is often accompanied by a loss of focus and initial motivation for pursuing certain goals. This, in turn, causes people to lose sight of purpose. If not addressed properly, burnout can lead to more serious mental and psychological issues like depression and/or anxiety. The following is a short list of some tangible tips to maintain a positive outlook and the motivation needed to reach goals.

Volunteering. Volunteering is a simple and effective way for students and adults of all backgrounds to feel gratitude and belonging. I have heard from many people, and have personally experienced, that volunteering is useful for putting one's own challenges into perspective. Over time, it can lead to a variety of other positive outcomes, including extra motivation to pursue one's goals, affirmation of triumph over one's challenges, and clarity toward purpose. When students volunteer, they are able to connect with people outside of their home and school environments, perhaps finding mentors or being able to serve as a mentor to others. Finally, volunteering enables people to see the different outcomes of their actions in self-affirming ways, which can also increase their agency.

Minding Mental Health. We are fortunate enough to live in an era when issues of mental health are becoming less stigmatized. Still, students need easy access to mental health resources on school grounds in K–12 and in college. Institutions that offer these resources should increase their visibility, further destigmatizing their use through greater awareness.

And, as we have discussed, students of color from low-income homes may often deal with multiple issues at home, from dealing with financial struggles to experiencing abuse. Mental health resources are important for improving a person's ability to cope with the different struggles in their lives. Again, all counselors—especially those working in lower-income neighborhoods—should be made aware of specific issues, such as trauma, that face the populations they encounter. Finally, young people should be taught skills and exercises they can practice on their own—such as mindfulness, meditation, or yoga—that help in attaining peace of mind. Some inner-city schools have made tremendous gains in student behavior and achievement by implementing mindfulness practices as a part of their curricula (George, 2016).

Positive Affirmation from Others, but also from the Self. Our students must receive support from different sources so they can eventually make meaningful investments in themselves and in society. All students, but especially those from socially and economically disadvantaged backgrounds, need access to strong mentorship. Mentoring can take many forms. Providing support groups for students and alumni is a simple way to create informal mentoring relationships. The Community College Honors program, which is where I met many of my participants, utilizes this approach. They hold weekly sessions for new students to meet informally, and for current students and alumni to stop by and share their perspectives. The sharing of experiences and challenges helps students navigate through similar challenges and achieve their goals. More importantly, it creates engagement and connection, and enables current students and alumni alike to realize they are not alone.

Beyond outside mentoring, it is helpful for people to give themselves positive affirmation. Simply put, it is important to nurture the ability to "not be too hard on oneself" on the journey of self-improvement and on the road to achieving goals. Perhaps most importantly, students need to avoid equating self-worth with achievement alone. That is not in the recipe for securing the inner peace needed to finding purpose and staying motivated. Sometimes inner peace requires celebrating how far you have come and also understanding that you are a work in progress. That leaves room for your agency to keep growing.

But, of course, remember to rely on others, especially good people who have your best interests in mind and at heart. Isolation is the enemy of agency and collaboration is at its core. So be there for others too, because in the end we are all in it together.

*

We do not know yet whether the Eric Garner rally or the hundreds of others that followed will bring about much lasting systemic change in our United States. The killings of Ahmaud Arbery, Breonna Taylor, and George Floyd in the spring of 2020 indicate we still have a long way to go. However, every time we see such unified actions they remind us of a very uniquely American tenacity. Our community-based responses showcase our ability to buckle down and persist *despite* challenges. Though I have been referring to this as "collective agency," maybe we could even call it a kind of *social grit*.

This is the strength and care we need to bring to education. A more equitable system and the resulting better-educated society are the most important investments we can make. When our students learn and flourish together, they make our communities more cohesive despite the differences that exist. They will also be more likely to meet one another on the front lines against the social problems that are inevitably ahead of us, many of which we have yet to imagine.

Together, we can live up to the challenge to treat education as our greatest collective responsibility. Our children depend on us to do so. And one day we will similarly depend on them. Let us give them the preparation they will need to eventually look after us all.

Positionality, Research Design, and Conceptual Framework

My experiences as an American, an academic, and an educator of color led me to develop the interests that guide this project. As a kid, I saw my parents' social mobility as we slowly moved from apartment complexes into a house in a predominantly White neighborhood in Portland, Oregon. I didn't have the words or concepts to describe how my life options improved as a result of the geographic change. I did know that the move was motivated by one thing: access to a better school system for my sister and me.

WHY I RESEARCH

In college, even though I studied prelaw, I wanted to write my senior thesis on youth gun violence surrounding Chicago Public Schools (CPS). It was my first experience doing my own research. I read Chicago history and gun laws, and interviewed CPS teachers and even a few Chicago Police Department (CPD) officers, including one commander. My paper opened the door to my first real job, working for the University of Chicago CrimeLab and Northwestern's Institute for Policy Research. As a research associate, my job included monitoring the intake process at the Cook County Juvenile Temporary Detention Center (JTDC), the largest of its kind in the country.

I saw the same kids return to the facility month after month, for extended stays, as they awaited trial for various crimes. The data showed that these kids mostly came from the South and West sides of Chicago, with a recidivism rate (likeliness to return to jail again) close to 90%. Some kids came back to the JTDC more than 10 times over the span of just a few years. Not surprisingly, most were chronically absent from school. I saw that many of them were intelligent in their own ways, reminding me that my life could have turned out much differently if my dad had not moved my family to the suburbs when I was a boy.

The following summer (2011), I moved east, to New York City. I came to get a master's in public administration from the NYU Wagner School for Public Service. Soon after I arrived, I found out that the New York City Department of Education was hiring an academic consultant. I was excited to take the job and move to a part-time schedule for my studies, thinking this could be my big break into the world of education. It was during the early days of Common Core, and New York was spearheading the national rollout. In addition to getting to work on the *Citywide Instructional Expectations*, a manual for the NYC schools, I also attended Principal Feedback Sessions, to hear how the school leaders were managing all the "new expectations."

One early morning I took the ferry to Staten Island and, with coffee in hand, I watched the Manhattan skyline reflecting in New York Harbor. The dozens of Staten Island principals who met us in the school library were already wide awake and had a clear, unified message: As always, they understood the need for new standards and "metrics," but what they needed was support and resources to be able to implement these changes while also empowering their teachers. I heard the same message in Brooklyn and the Bronx. Even though I was there representing the system—their supposed caretaker—I couldn't help but agree with what they were saying about not being cared for enough.

Years later, to be honest, I'm not really sure what kind of help and resources they actually got. I'm also not sure that the full responsibility to provide support to the schools rests solely on the government. After all, the government works for us. Ultimately, *we* have to care about the education of other people's children to make it more effective.

One spring day after work, I decided to take the train up two stops to attend a lecture by Pedro Noguera at NYU. In my notes I wrote: "According to International PISA Scores, the U.S. ranks in the 20s for overall student achievement. If you control for poverty and look at U.S. scores in the wealthiest 25 percent of communities, then the U.S. ranks in the top 3. 'Schools can't solve social problems themselves.' Dr. Noguera" (3/28/12).

That small event may have changed the direction of my life. Afterward, I went up to Pedro and introduced myself. I had been on the waitlist to get into the sociology of education doctoral program but was not sure if I wanted to leave my DOE job and the master's program. But when I eventually got the call to take the only spot offered that year, I felt compelled to do so.

These experiences and many others each day continue to shape my views on the limits and possibilities of education. And though I am often in awe of schools and districts doing excellent work in the face of the structural limitations they encounter, I now believe more strongly than ever that the greatest imperfection in our democracy is that a child's future can be largely determined by the zip code they are born into. This is what we are collectively up against. Through research I want to help people with power to make more informed decisions, but I also want to share stories that allow us to better understand the complex realities of other people.

Positive change is boundless, but only if we can keep in mind what Alicia insisted on: "Every human being is in fact a human being and should be treated as such. . . . [Humans] are absolutely wonderful and capable and brilliant."

RESEARCH POSITIONALITY

Morrell (2004) says that it is close to impossible to remove oneself fully from one's subject matter, especially in qualitative work. The questions we ask and the conclusions we draw are often, if just partially, related to our own social contexts and experiences. It is not necessarily as important to be "value neutral" as it is to consider your role in supporting or rejecting certain arguments (Morrell, 2004). I can readily admit that my own background likely played a small role in how I interpret some of my data. At the same time, being a man of color around the same age as many of my participants may have given me an ability to create a comfortable environment for them to open up in.

In some ways, I connected to participants on a more insider level. I have had some firsthand experience with microaggressions similar to those they may have encountered and described, though I generally refrained from adding to the conversation. Some might contest this connection as an issue in education or other research because they favor a more removed position to avoid bias. But proximity has benefits in interviewing because subjects might feel more inclined to be honest (Mercer, 2007). In trying to understand differences, a researcher might subconsciously "other" their subjects from themselves (Canales, 2000). I sometimes experienced the opposite. I was reminded of my upbringing as a brown child who had to reconcile different identities and navigate the dominant White cultural context.

I described my stance to my participants when I met them: I sought to learn about their achievements and challenges with hopes of creating more equitable environments for youth who experience disadvantage and marginalization. In turn, they opened up to me about their "gravest fears, deepest traumas, and unguarded ambitions" (Kundu, 2018, p. 76). I commit to respecting their identities and personhood, and therefore I have de-identified all of them throughout this book. I hope that giving some voice to traditionally underrepresented individuals contributes to a more comprehensive understanding of constructs that can oppress similar groups (hooks, 1992; Morrell, 2004).

METHODOLOGY

For this project I used sociological methods. I collected, transcribed, and coded my interviews using an inductive research process to organize and analyze my data. The people in my sample faced serious challenges that can prevent many from rising up the social ladder toward family-sustaining, professional careers. My intention was primarily to develop different hypotheses about what types of factors, supports, environments, and relationships can help students with disadvantages achieve academically and professionally. This project was foremost "hypothesis-generating"—the themes I describe are meant to be further studied—I was not determined to uncover large trends or generalize largely about why some populations achieve and others do not, more than I wanted to consider these cases.

My research confirmed that agency and grit, as currently conceived in education research, were, in fact, to an extent, relevant to these narratives of success. At the same time, my study challenges some commonly accepted ideas on achievement. I developed my own theories around goal formation, college and career, and mobility, building on those that exist and are respected in my field. My findings chapters (Chapters 3 through 5) show some ways that individuals can navigate and triumph over the various personal, structural, and institutional challenges they may encounter in their lives.

Qualitative research is critical for understanding the internal contexts and the rationales that guide people's behavior. By collecting data directly from interactions with participants, I positioned myself to better understand the meanings they assigned to the choices they claimed to make (Rubin & Rubin, 2011). My research contributes to a (hopefully) growing field that focuses on how marginalized students' narratives can make space for their often-absent voices to inform the very research that assess them.

To better prepare myself to uncover factors that are facilitative of these successes, I turned to classic and current theories on student success and achievement contexts. Existing literature in the sociology of education, positive psychology, and the psychology of education guided me to a starting point, a hypothesis that *agency* and *grit* both somehow interacted and contributed to observable patterns between participants' stories. Both agency and grit are well-researched subjects, but until my study began (more than 4 years ago) I had not seen them considered in the dialectical fashion in which I present them here (refer to my Conceptual Framework, depicted in Figures 1.2 and 1.3 of Chapter 1) to understand the achievement of exceptional students. Today, these topics are often discussed together in research that assesses people's abilities and mobility (see Hitlin & Kwon, 2016; Kwon, 2017, for a good discussion on competencies, control, and mobility).

Of course, a completely thorough comprehension or mastery of how these concepts operate in students' lives, and exist in the broader context of education, cannot be obtained from this single project. Nor are we as scholars yet close to a full understanding of how certain behaviors and their interactions allow some students to flourish and others not; many of these concepts are in fact invisible to the naked eye and hard to identify. For example, there continues to be some confusion about the differences between resilience and grit, and I myself continue to see more similarities between agency and grit the more I learn about them.

However, the specific questions that guided my simple study were mostly answerable through the conceptual framework I created. I more clearly understand why studying behavior without also considering elements of social life gives only a limited perspective of goal-setting, achievement, and mobility; the same applies for research on the structural conditions of social life that fail to consider the importance of behaviors. I hope this research can, to a small extent, enrich the ongoing sociological discussions on the influence of human agency and structural forces. Having provided an interdisciplinary example between the sociology of education and concepts rooted in positive psychology, I specifically contribute to a narrow body of work that seeks to learn about how students can succeed despite social and economic obstacles.

Interviews

My interviews ran for about 75 minutes on average, in which my participants spoke for approximately 80%–90% of the recorded time. I created a small, semistructured interview protocol to allow for following natural trends and the direction of dialogue the participants went in (Rubin & Rubin, 2011). This format allowed me to be flexible and follow emerging ideas in the moment, though each interview started with the same root questions (Underwood, Satterthwait, & Bartlett, 2010).

Due to the sensitive nature of the topics we discussed, I made the effort to assume a natural, conversational approach that encouraged participants to feel at ease. Perhaps this is why participants seemed open to disclosing parts of their lives they might keep more guarded. I have had formal and extensive training in conducting both highly structured interviews and semistructured interviews (I have done nearly 200 interviews to date). As such, I aimed to go in a different direction for this project in order to give my participants more control over the interview. Very structured interviews can have a rigid feel, which to me sometimes seems like having predetermined motives or desired findings. As a result of my method, my findings were quite broad, which is why my findings chapters are presented in such broad-bucket sections—my participants and I really did talk a little bit about everything.

My interviews all started with open-ended questions such as, "Describe who you are as a person. What are some of the most important characteristics about you that you would like someone to notice?" (Kundu, 2018, p.

91). If these questions were too difficult, or if the participant stumbled, I reworded, perhaps using, "Let's say you're at a party where you haven't met anyone. What are some of the first things you would say to a person, when introducing yourself?" (p. 91). This helped to break the ice and set a friendly tone for the interview. I asked why they described themselves that way, and where specifically these qualities came from. This started the deeper dive into my participants' life histories—they eventually described their families, upbringings, neighborhoods, home countries, and why they seem to be the people they are today (p. 91).

I slowly pivoted to education in each interview. I asked questions similar to, "Were you *always* good at school . . . did you enjoy it?" (Kundu, 2018, p. 91). This helped me to gain information on their school environments, families, mentors, and the different values they placed on education. Many participants found refuge in controlling their academic achievements and excelling scholastically; others hated or resented school for long periods of time. Most had substantial shifts about how they thought about school, which helped them see education as important in producing benefits and economic outcomes. I asked questions like, "How did this change come to be? Did you notice yourself changing? Do you keep in touch with that teacher or mentor, and do you think she realizes her impact on you?" (p. 92).

Eventually I asked all participants to place themselves in a different context, one out of their lives. For instance, "Let's say someone else had to overcome that feeling of helplessness you did, and give college another try. How would you teach them to do what you did, or, what would you tell them is important to consider? What is something you would tell someone as advice, if they were experiencing the same struggles as you?" (Kundu, 2018, p. 92). These questions provided me with some insight on how participants think about the structures and constructs that surround them.

I also sought to learn about their daily lives. If they mentioned mental health being important in their life, I asked what practices they utilized to maintain positive mental health despite feeling down. These questions also probed at agency and grit in a sense as I learned their larger values and outlook. I asked broad questions, such as, "What is one of the most important lessons you have learned in life?" (Kundu, 2018, p. 93). I thus learned about my participants' hardships related to growing up poor, often hungry, at times homeless; without two-parent households, sometimes with neglectful or abusive parents; trauma; and much more. I learned about their ability to maintain optimism and faith; to find positive reinforcement; to stay determined, focused, and humble; and about how they located trust, inner selflessness, and grit.

Before all interviews, I informed participants that interviews would be recorded and that I would keep them anonymous in whatever I published. They were encouraged to choose their own aliases, and a little more than half did so; for others, I came up with aliases. I interviewed the first participant in December 2015 and conducted my last interview in January 2017; I transcribed interviews during this period as well, usually within a couple weeks of the interview.

I also took notes and analytical memos shortly after each interview while the experience and emotions were fresh in my mind. To reduce my data, I created page-long memos that summarized my primary takeaways, connecting each new interview with those that preceded it (Griffee, 2005; Miles, Huberman, & Saldana, 2013). After doing my first 10 interviews, the memos started to connect themes between and across interviews. For example, after interviewing Malcolm, whom I met a month or so after I met Stan, I wrote:

> Malcolm uses analogies similar to how Stan described life's hardships as miniscule, compared to the difficulties others have to deal with. Malcolm says, "I've got my kid next to me, air in my lungs, what do I have to complain about?" Both of these men show what can be described as an *overcompensating resilience* for growing up without a father figure in their lives. At the same time, both of these young men are very involved fathers themselves. (Kundu, 2018, pp. 95–96)

Then, I logged the idea of "overcompensating resilience" as a category, which could potentially develop into a larger, thematic finding, depending on how much this idea resurfaced in other interviews and continued to appear significant.

I formally coded interviews using Dedoose research software. I analyzed data in three main phases: coding, charting, and mapping/interpretation. My Venn diagram in Chapter 1 and my initial codes of "grit" and "agency," resulted from an inductive research process and general hypotheses (and investigation of literature) on these subjects (Ary, Jacobs, Irvine, & Walker, 2013). Refer to my Conceptual Framework in Chapter 1 (see Figures 1.2 and 1.3) to see what kinds of characteristics I looked for to locate either trait. From my transcripts I began to identify patterns of both adaptive mindsets and forms of resistance that participants described (Garner & Scott, 2013; Gilligan, 2015; Rosenbloom & Way, 2004). I completed log entries in an Excel spreadsheet, recording date, time, alias, race, age, and any important details about my participants.

Participant Selection Criteria and Recruitment

I created a sample pool that matched the broader population of youth and students in New York City public schools in regard to race, income, and immigration status. I was able to place the experiences of my participants in a wider context required for inductive methods to extrapolate and consider how my findings would be relevant to a larger, but similar, population. To operationalize my use of "experiencing success," I selected participants who matched at least one of the following characteristics, which are traditionally associated with academic success and social mobility: "(a) Individuals currently enrolled in, registering into, or graduated from a 4-year college granting a traditional bachelor's degree; (b) individuals currently enrolled in an associate's degree program with plans to attend and acceptance into a bachelor's degree program; (c) individuals who have graduated with at least a bachelor's degree and are currently working in a highly professionalized career track (e.g., law, medicine, government, engineering, finance) or pursuing a graduate-level degree" (Kundu, 2018, p. 78).

My sample included 50 participants, consisting of equal numbers of male ($n = 25$) and female ($n = 25$) participants. Forty-eight participants identified as people of color, which is the population I intended to recruit. Two did not identify. Forty-four of the participants were between the ages of 18 and 29 years old and in the "emerging adulthood" space (Arnett, 2014). Studying this age range is relevant to researching people who are beginning to explore many different possibilities in their life, and it may provide a sense of trends and cultural values that the future of the United States will exhibit (Arnett, 2014; Arum & Roksa, 2014).

My participants' aliases, races, ages, and "traditional factors associated with risk" (TFAR) are recorded in Table A.1, sorted by age.[1] During certain instances in my data analysis, I categorized by gender to see if it would reveal any gender-specific commonalities among these participants; for instance, men were less likely to use the word "trauma" in describing experiences in their life. However, for the themes discussed in this book, I do not make any gender-related distinctions, and thus the data are displayed together. Table A.2 presents the key for translating the TFAR acronyms. For example, if a participant experienced homelessness during any period in their life, I recorded it as "HO"; "TV" or "Trauma, Violent" can indicate having experienced physical abuse from a parent, bullying in school, or gang violence. For example, participant MP was once beaten and stabbed multiple times by a group of men, likely in a gang, when he was with his friend late one night.

"Family issues" may indicate that a participant grew up in a physically or emotionally abusive household. "Immigrant story" represents that a participant is a first-generation immigrant, perhaps leaving family from the native country, or having undocumented status and barriers to educational opportunities. "Child at young age" is used for the participants who had children before the age of 18, most often leading to single parenting. These factors were recorded given the extent of what my participants felt comfortable disclosing to me. This is why some participants do not have TFAR variables listed by their name; even though there is a likelihood that they experienced one or more of these challenges, they did not explicitly mention it in our interview and I did not assume.

Table A.1. Participants

Alias	Race	Age	TFAR
Camila	Latinx	19	SM, MH
Mario	Latinx (Dominican)	20	SF, TV
Chris	Latinx and White	20	DR, FA, MH
Sari	Latinx (Dominican)	20	MH, SM
Penny	Latinx (Dominican)	20	IN
Maggie	Latinx and Filipino	20	IM, MH
Alicia	Black	20	MH
Isabella	Latinx	20	FA, MH
Brittni	Black	20	ED
Humaira	Latinx	20	
Joe	Latinx	21	HO, SM, MH
Brian	Filipino	21	MI
Princess	Latinx (Dominican)	21	FA, MH, IM
Imperial	Black	22	SM
Mario	Latinx	21	GA, IN, MH
Liz	Latinx (Dominican)	22	IM
Glenn	Black	22	GA, IN
Gabby	Latinx	23	FA, TS
Mohammad	Black	24	
Linda	Latinx	24	TV
Sasha	Black	24	
MP	Black	25	SM, TV, MH
Drew	Black	25	IM
Bob	Black	25	
Winchester	Latinx (Dominican)	25	FA, TV
Rose	Latinx	25	FA, HO, TV, MH
Stephanie	Latinx	25	FA, MH
Sasha	Black	25	
J-Stud	Black	26	ED, SM, MH
Nadira	Latinx and Asian	26	DR, MH
Jonny	Black	26	IN, TV, MH
Gouvia	Black	26	FA
Malcolm	Black	27	HO, FM, SM, TV

(continued)

Table A.1. Participants (continued)

Alias	Race	Age	TFAR
Stan	Black	27	CH, HO
Bayete	Latinx	27	IN
Moe	Black	27	CH, FA, HO, TV
Roxanne	Black	27	CH, SM
Tara	Black	27	MH
Omar	Latinx	28	IM
Xavier	Black (Dominican)	29	GA, IN, SM, TV
Sunny	Black	29	SM
Winny	-	29	FA, HO, MH, SM
Vanessa	Black and Latinx	29	CH, DR, FA, ED
Hector	Latinx	27	MH
Edwin	Latinx	30	IM, SM
Jenie	-	30	DR
Frida	Latinx	30	SM
Tyrique	Latinx	35	GA, IM, IN
Andrea	Black	35	FA, TS, TV
JLo	Black	40	CH, DR

Table A.2. Risk Factors

Acronym	Traditional Factor Associated with Risk (TFAR)
CH	Had child as a teenager
DR	Struggled with substance/drug abuse
ED	Educational issues in K–12
FA	Family issues
GA	Gang involvement
HO	Homelessness
IM	Immigrant story
IN	Incarceration story
MH	Mental health issue
SF	Single-father household
SM	Single-mother household
TS	Trauma, Sexual
TV	Trauma, Violent

My participants all grew up in low-resource New York neighborhoods during their formative years. "This includes students from Hunts Point, Bronx (where the average median household income was $21,366) or Brownsville ($20,640) (Furman Center for Real Estate and Urban Policy, 2017); and some similar Queens neighborhoods. Four participants grew up in Manhattan, specifically in low-income homes in Harlem" (Kundu, 2018, p. 83).

"Every participant either: (a) attended schools in New York City for their K–12 education, (b) attended or is currently attending a community college in New York State, or (c) has graduated from or is currently attending a college in New York State" (Kundu, 2018, pp. 83–84). The participants are quite exceptional given that other students who grow up with the same levels of family income are not, on average, able to find such academic and professional success. Most of them experienced challenges in life that middle-class children are usually able to avoid: incarceration, gang involvement, dropping out of high school, substance abuse or parents with substance abuse problems, single-parent households, and becoming pregnant in their early teens.

Students who experience these social disadvantages also often encounter racial or cultural prejudice. I make the additional claim that "socially disadvantaged" students do not have access to strong social capital, which for many others connects them to higher education or employment. "Economically disadvantaged" students qualify for the National School Lunch Program and receive free or reduced-price school meals (Schacter & Jo, 2005). Each person in this study meets these qualifications for being socially and economically disadvantaged.

I recruited people for my study with the help of two after-school programs that help to send New York City high school students to college, through rigorous enrichment programs. These programs select students by the same need-based criteria described previously. "At the time of their interview, all participants had graduated from these programs. They were attending a bachelor's-degree granting institution, or had graduated with their bachelor's and working in a professionalized field. Alternatively, some were attending graduate-level study (Kundu, 2018).

ADDRESSING LIMITATIONS AND LOOKING FORWARD

As with all research, my study has limitations, and I want to address some of the main ones here. My sample was diverse in some ways, but within it there were many shared characteristics in regard to race, age group, traditional factors associated with risk, and challenges experienced. Studying a more thoroughly homogenous sample would have allowed me to specifically learn more about the effects of one variable, such as the effects of having a single mother or of unexpected teenage pregnancy. However, at the onset I was more interested in how, broadly, students of color from low-income backgrounds form academic and professional goals despite obstacles. I was hoping to find some useful information about what kinds of factors can help students navigate challenges on their way to success. Ideally, these insights on what is possible might help a broader range of students who experience poverty and other circumstances of birth that are *outside* of their control.

Some researchers would correctly point out that in the scheme of qualitative work, this was a relatively smaller-scale study. Fifty participants is not a very large sample. Some favor larger samples in the name of rigor, skeptical about sampling bias and the potential for overoccurrence and underoccurrence of certain themes. This is a limitation that I have been mindful of since I conceived this project and laid it on a reasonable timeline. I will thus also be the first to admit that any more peculiar findings would benefit from further investigation and the inclusion of more participants. Because of this, as I stated much earlier, I do not intend to make claims that my thematic findings apply to *all* low-income students of color who have experienced similar disadvantages.

Still, I feel comfortable with how I have presented my data and shared what I have learned. I aimed to not venture too far to contend anything as axiomatic based on this work, avoiding overgeneralizing statements about similar populations of students. I presented my findings broadly, almost shying away from any controversial lines. Some may, of course, take issue with that, perhaps rightfully. But for the most part, it would be hard to argue with ideas that having strong-willed guardians who care about the virtues of civic responsibility are good, or that many minority students can overwork themselves to states of burnout without adequate social support. I am happy to have those debates with anyone who feels the need.

Finally, two issues about collection and representation may emerge about my project. Due to "social desirability," some may say that my participants could have said things that they thought I wanted to hear (Grimm, 2010). Or, secondly, that I was biased in my data selection and presentation, showing only the best and most "juicy" stories. For the former issue, I have to reiterate the context of these interviews. Participants discussed sensitive topics, such as trauma, with me, a researcher who was a complete stranger to them. I do not believe there can be "hoped for" answers. We spoke about a wide range of topics to the extent that these individuals felt comfortable as they discussed their former and ongoing challenges in life. We developed trust, and therefore there is much that I have not shared here. For example, one of my larger findings revolved around how individuals can slowly overcome being raised by guardians who were abusive or harmfully neglectful. I may someday publish work on that topic when I best figure out how to do so with the delicate respect that topic deserves.

To avoid data-representation bias, I used an in-depth coding scheme that stayed true to inductive research methods, uncovering new themes and building on old ones slowly over time. The quotes I used here best represent to me the larger thematic findings I wanted to discuss. You will notice that many participants, though represented in my chart, were not included explicitly in this work. I hope that I best represented them, too, through the quotes I ended up having to choose from. My goal was to describe some factors that allow some individuals to become exceptional and triumph in ways we should hope other students can. *That* was the main commonality among the people I sampled: They are each compelling in many ways.

For future research, I am excited to extend these basic premises to other projects. It would be valuable to recruit more students, from suburban and rural communities, with the same research question to learn more about these topics, not just in urban environments. I truly believe it is always a worthwhile endeavor to learn from the success of people who have overcome various difficulties, in order to help others who may experience similarities. These asset-based approaches allow us as scholars to not only identify a problem but also contemplate potential solutions. I recently published in *The Urban Review* (Kundu, 2019) on college burnout based on this research, but with half of the paper focusing on how students can *overcome* and reignite their motivations because this is largely an issue of college retention. It is in these simple ways that we can expand notions of what is possible for our students.

I encourage and appreciate any researchers who apply similar (or even the same) research questions in order to learn about factors and influences that can help our students thrive. Too often, we ask why certain students fail to achieve or climb the social ladder, potentially furthering implicit biases and deficit perspectives. If instead we ask how diverse populations with various challenges can learn to thrive, we open ourselves up to the ability to learn and improve systems from these stories. I hope that readers have gained something on the theoretical, practical, and modern relevance of agency as a sociological concept; that through these examples, they now better understand how certain systems of support and opportunities can foster agency despite structural obstacles; and that they realize that environmental factors go hand-in-hand with behavioral traits such as grit, and that we must consider both to help students achieve success.

Notes

Prologue

1. Noam Chomsky has often spoken out against inequality and has directly critiqued *The Bell Curve*.

2. There is some contention about whether Mark Twain or Grant Allen (a contemporary writer of Twain's) deserves more credit for this quote, because both have been reported using variations of it.

3. As reported by the *Washington Post*, Obama and George W. Bush both called education the "civil rights issue of our time," a sentiment that Trump echoed in his February 28, 2017, Joint Address to Congress (Brown, 2017).

Introduction

1. In Chapter 3, I discuss how students who have unexpectedly become young, single parents can thrive academically and professionally, if provided certain social and cultural supports.

2. Of course, having also been a "workforce development" researcher for some time now, I am a big proponent of vocational and career and technical education (CTE). Associate's degrees and trade credentials can be immensely beneficial in helping some people enter into an occupation that earns a family-sustaining income. At the same time, I am fearful of the economic implications of constantly rising college tuition and incessant student loan debts. But for the purposes of this research, and while acknowledging how hard getting into college is for some student populations, I am using this definition here.

Chapter 2

1. When I shared with my wife that my interviewees picked their own aliases, she told me that giving them the freedom to choose their name seems like granting them a form of agency. It was a nice surprise to realize that I subconsciously internalized and used some lessons from my ongoing research.

2. In terms of qualitative research, I have conducted more than 200 interviews to date (with students, school staff, and other education professionals around the country), but the 50 included in this book are the ones that focused on understanding student agency.

3. In the Appendix, you will find the tables that display these participants' aliases, race, ages, and abbreviated risk factors. I used acronyms for the challenges experienced by participants with the intention to provide a quick visual account of them.

Chapter 3

1. I will elaborate on the idea of "not having a childhood," especially in Alicia's story, in which she describes taking on many adult responsibilities as a child.

Chapter 4

1. Figures 1.2 and 1.3 in Chapter 1 give examples of a couple forms of cultural competency that I have found beneficial to students through my work.

Chapter 5

1. Similar to Brian, it was public speaking, through joining the high school speech and debate team, that allowed me to break out of my shell. Speaking in front of others allowed me to see a different side of myself and to this day remains one of my favorite ways to challenge myself.

2. Scholarship in positive psychology aligns with Alicia's positive mindset. It views individuals at a constant point of potential and not deficiency.

3. Refer to my Conceptual Framework diagram (see Figures 1.2 and 1.3) to see how attention to a student's genuine interests serve as cultural capital to help them become engaged. This is depicted in J-Stud's story, in which he describes how a high school mentor bonded with him over his interest in music and eventually helped him buy into his academic work.

4. Volunteering is an excellent way to fulfill our collective responsibilities to help each child. I elaborate on the importance of volunteer work in the Conclusion chapter (Chapter 6). For those of us who have been lucky enough to grow up more fortunate than others, volunteering allows a proxy to gaining these deep insights while also fostering our own agency and grit.

Chapter 6

1. Federally collected data on police shootings that were fatal, between 2010 and 2012, revealed that young Black men were 21 times likelier to be killed than their White counterparts (Gabrielson, Sagara, & Jones, 2014). I would contend that we are not living in a postracial world yet.

2. I originally believed that I might use this passage as the opening for my book, but over the years I felt unsure how it might apply to a book about supporting vulnerable students. Now, I have come to see these topics as more interconnected than ever before. Education is the largest tool for empowerment we have.

3. Learn more about New York City's Outward Bound programs at www.ny-coutwardbound.org/about-us/our-approach/

4. Imperial's story about how formative it was to have mentors from NYU visit his high school to teach SAT prep is a great illustration of this.

5. There is a clear and longstanding "psychological" perspective on suicide. Durkheim showed that suicide is associated with feeling disconnected to social groups and lacking social cohesion. Similarly, I describe burnout as being a social problem that manifests internally and individually.

6. Unfortunately, the SYEP was suspended for the summer of 2020 due to the impact of COVID-19. This has caused many hopeful young people from low-income homes to lose out on summer work and the opportunity to contribute to their families' income. This serves as an example of how structural problems can impact some communities harder than others.

Appendix

1. I still take issue with the use and definition of "risk factors" as traditionally identified in people of color from low socioeconomic status (SES) backgrounds. I believe this category presents a problematic association and predetermination of people with lower abilities to excel. For instance, rather than seeing unplanned pregnancy as an event connected solely to delinquency, I see it as an opportunity to intervene and help to put a student on an improved life trajectory.

References

Abel, J. R., & Deitz, R. (2014). Do the benefits of college still outweigh the costs? *Current Issues in Economics and Finance, 20*(3), 1–12.

Ainsworth-Darnell, J. W., & Downey, D. B. (1998). Assessing the oppositional culture explanation for racial/ethnic differences in school performance. *American Sociological Review, 63*(4), 536–553.

Althusser, L. (1971). Ideology and state apparatuses (Notes towards an investigation). In L. Althusser (Ed.), *Lenin and philosophy and other essays* (pp. 171–174). New York, NY: Monthly Review Press.

Amato, P. R., & Keith, B. (1991). Parental divorce and the well-being of children: A meta-analysis. *Psychological Bulletin, 110*(1), 26.

Anderson, C., & Sally, D. (2013). *The numbers game: Why everything you know about soccer is wrong.* New York, NY: Penguin.

Annie E. Casey Foundation, & Center for the Study of Social Policy. (2019). *Kids count data book.* Washington, DC: Center for the Study of Social Policy.

Arnett, J. J. (2001). Conceptions of the transition to adulthood: Perspectives from adolescence through midlife. *Journal of Adult Development, 8*(2), 133–143.

Arnett, J. J. (2014). *Emerging adulthood: The winding road from the late teens through the twenties.* New York, NY: Oxford University Press.

Arum, R. (2005). *Judging school discipline.* Cambridge, MA: Harvard University Press.

Arum, R., & Roksa, J. (2014). *Aspiring adults adrift: Tentative transitions of college graduates.* Chicago, IL: University of Chicago Press.

Ary, D., Jacobs, L. C., Irvine, C. K. S., & Walker, D. (2013). *Introduction to research in education* (9th ed.). Boston, MA: Cengage.

Aslam, R. W., Hendry, M., Booth, A., Carter, B., Charles, J. M., Craine, N., . . . Whitaker, R. (2017). Intervention now to eliminate repeat unintended pregnancy in teenagers (INTERUPT): A systematic review of intervention effectiveness and cost-effectiveness, and qualitative and realist synthesis of implementation factors and user engagement. *BMC Medicine, 15*(1), article 155.

Auguste, B. G., Hancock, B., & Laboissière, M. (2009). The economic cost of the US education gap. *The McKinsey Quarterly, 2*, 1–4.

Baker, E. L., & O'Neil, H. F. (2016). The intersection of international achievement testing and educational policy development. In L. Volante (Ed.), *Global perspectives on large-scale reform* (pp. 122–140), New York, NY: Routledge.

Ballenger, C. (1999). *Teaching other people's children: Literacy and learning in a bilingual classroom.* New York, NY: Teachers College Press.

Bandura, A. (1977). Self-efficacy: Toward a unifying theory of behavioral change. *Psychological Review, 84*(2), 191–215. doi:10.1037/0033–295X.84.2.191

Bandura, A. (1982). Self-efficacy mechanism in human agency. *American Psychologist, 37*(2), 122–147.

Bandura, A. (1986). The explanatory and predictive scope of self-efficacy theory. *Journal of Social and Clinical Psychology, 4*(3), 359–373.

Bandura, A. (1997). *Self-efficacy: The exercise of control.* New York, NY: W. H. Freeman.

Bandura, A. (2006). Guide for constructing self-efficacy scales. *Self-efficacy Beliefs of Adolescents, 5*(1), 307–337.

Barcelos, C. A., & Gubrium, A. C. (2014). Reproducing stories: Strategic narratives of teen pregnancy and motherhood. *Social Problems, 61*(3), 466–481.

Barker, C. (2003). *Cultural studies: Theory and practice.* Thousand Oaks, CA: Sage.

Bartlett, L., & García, O. (2011). *Additive schooling in subtractive times: Bilingual education and Dominican immigrant youth in the Heights.* Nashville, TN: Vanderbilt University Press.

Bidwell, C. E., & Friedkin, N. E. (1988). *The sociology of education.* Newbury Park, CA: Sage.

Blankstein, A. M., Noguera, P., & Kelly, L. (2016). Excellence through equity: Five principles of courageous leadership to guide achievement for every student. Alexandria, VA: ASCD.

Blaska, J. (1993). The power of language: Speak and write using "person first." *Perspectives on Disability, 4*(4), 25–32.

Boas, F. (1940). *Race, language, and culture.* Chicago, IL: University of Chicago Press.

Bonilla-Silva, E. (2010). *Racism without racists: Color-blind racism & racial inequality in contemporary America.* Lanham, MD: Rowman & Littlefield.

Bowles, S., & Gintis, H. (1976). *Schooling in capitalist America.* New York, NY: Basic Books.

Bowles, S., & Gintis, H. (2011). *A cooperative species: Human reciprocity and its evolution.* Princeton, NJ: Princeton University Press.

Bourdieu, P. (1974). The school as a conservative force: Scholastic and cultural inequalities. *Contemporary Research in the Sociology of Education, 32,* 46.

Bourdieu, P. (1986). The forms of capital. In J. G. Richardson (Ed.), *Handbook of theory and research for the sociology of education* (pp. 241–258). New York, NY: Greenwood Press.

Bourdieu, P., & Passeron, J. C. (1977). *Reproduction in education, culture and society.* Thousand Oaks, CA: Sage.

Bourdieu, P., & Passeron, J. C. (1990). *Reproduction in education, society and culture* (Vol. 4). Thousand Oaks, CA: Sage.

Boyatzis, R. E., Smith, M. L., & Beveridge, A. J. (2010). Coaching with compassion: Inspiring health, well-being, and development in organizations. *Journal of Applied Behavioral Science, 49*(2), 153–178.

Boykin, A. W., & Noguera, P. (2011). *Creating the opportunity to learn: Moving from research to practice to close the achievement gap.* Alexandria, VA: ASCD.

Brand, J. E., & Xie, Y. (2010). Who benefits most from college? Evidence for negative selection in heterogeneous economic returns to higher education. *American Sociological Review, 75*(2), 273–302.

Brody, G. H., Yu, T., Chen, E., Beach, S. R., & Miller, G. E. (2016). Family-centered prevention ameliorates the longitudinal association between risky family processes and epigenetic aging. *Journal of Child Psychology and Psychiatry, 57*(5), 566–574.

Bronfenbrenner, K. (2009, May 20). *No holds barred: The intensification of employer opposition to organizing* (Briefing Paper No. 235). Washington, DC: Economic Policy Institute.

Brown, E. (2017, February 28). Obama also called education the "civil rights issue of our time." *The Washington Post.* Retrieved from www.washingtonpost.com/politics/2017/live-updates/trump-white-house/real-time-fact-checking-and-analysis-of-trumps-address-to-congress/obama-also-called-education-the-civil-rights-issue-of-our-time/

Byrd, D. R., & McKinney, K. J. (2012). Individual, interpersonal, and institutional level factors associated with the mental health of college students. *Journal of American College Health, 60*(3), 185–193.

Canales, M. K. (2000). Othering: Toward an understanding of difference. *Advances in Nursing Science, 22*(4), 16–31.

Carey, R. L. (2016). "Keep that in mind . . . You're gonna go to college": Family influence on the college going processes of Black and Latino high school boys. *The Urban Review, 48*(5), 718–742.

Carnoy, M., & Levin, H. (1985). *Schooling and work in the democratic state.* Redwood City, CA: Stanford University Press.

Carter, P. L. (2003). "Black" cultural capital, status positioning, and schooling conflicts for low-income African American youth. *Social Problems, 50*(1), 136–15.

Carter, P. L., & Welner, K. G. (Eds.). (2013). *Closing the opportunity gap: What America must do to give every child an even chance.* New York, NY: Oxford University Press.

Centers for Disease Control and Prevention. (2018, January 26). Mental health – Home page. Retrieved from www.cdc.gov/mentalhealth/index.htm

Chavous, T. M. (2005). An intergroup contact-theory framework for evaluating racial climate on predominantly White college campuses. *American Journal of Community Psychology, 36*(3–4), 239–257.

Cherng, H. Y. S., & Halpin, P. F. (2016). The importance of minority teachers: Student perceptions of minority versus White teachers. *Educational Researcher, 45*(7), 407–420.

Chetty, R., Hendren, N., Jones, M. R., & Porter, S. R. (2018). *Race and economic opportunity in the United States: An intergenerational perspective* (Report No. w24441). Cambridge, MA: National Bureau of Economic Research.

Cholewa, B., Goodman, R. D., West-Olatunji, C., & Amatea, E. (2014). A qualitative examination of the impact of culturally responsive educational practices on the psychological well-being of students of color. *The Urban Review, 46*(4), 574–596.

Chua, A. (2011). *Battle hymn of the tiger mother.* New York, NY: Bloomsbury.

Chua, A., & Rubenfeld, J. (2014). *The triple package: How three unlikely traits explain the rise and fall of cultural groups in America.* New York, NY: Penguin.

Clausen, J. A., & Jones, C. J. (1998). Predicting personality stability across the life span: The role of competence and work and family commitments. *Journal of Adult Development, 5*(2), 73–83.

Clear, J. (2018). *Atomic habits: An easy & proven way to build good habits & break bad ones.* New York, NY: Penguin.

Cohen, C. J. (2010). *Democracy remixed: Black youth and the future of American politics.* New York, NY: Oxford University Press.

Coleman, J. S. (2000). Social capital in the creation of human capital. In E. L. Lesser (Ed.), *Knowledge and social capital: Foundations and applications* (pp. 17–41). Woburn, MA: Butterworth-Heinemann.

Coleman, J. S., Campbell, E., Hobson, C., McPartland, J., Mood, A., Weinfeld, F., & York, R. (1966). *Equality of educational opportunity* (Report No. OE-38001). Washington, DC: National Center for Educational Statistics.

Collins, J. (1988). Language and class in minority education. *Anthropology & Education Quarterly, 19*(4), 299–32

Collins, R. (2002). Credential inflation and the future of universities. In S. Brint (Ed.), *The future of the city of intellect: The changing American university* (pp. 23–46.) Palo Alto, CA: Stanford University Press.

Comstock, D. L., Hammer, T. R., Strentzsch, J., Cannon, K., Parsons, J., & Salazar, G. (2008). Relational-cultural theory: A framework for bridging relational, multicultural, and social justice competencies. *Journal of Counseling & Development, 86*, 279–287.

Conchas, G. Q., Lin, A. R., Oseguera, L., & Drake, S. J. (2015). Superstar or scholar? African American male youths' perceptions of opportunity in a time of change. *Urban Education, 50*(6), 660–688.

Creswell, J. D., Welch, W. T., Taylor, S. E., Sherman, D. K., Gruenewald, T. L., & Mann, T. (2005). Affirmation of personal values buffers neuroendocrine and psychological stress responses. *Psychological Science, 16*(11), 846–851.

Darling-Hammond, L. (2010). Teacher education and the American future. *Journal of Teacher Education, 61*(1–2), 35–47.

Davis-Kean, P. E. (2005). The influence of parent education and family income on child achievement: The indirect role of parental expectations and the home environment. *Journal of Family Psychology, 19*(2), 294.

DeAngelo, L., Franke, R. Hurtado, S. Pryor, J. H. & Tran, S. (2011). *Completing college: Assessing graduation rates at four-year institutions.* Los Angeles, CA: Higher Education Research Institute at UCLA.

Delpit, L. D. (2012). *"Multiplication is for white people": Raising expectations for other people's children.* New York, NY: The New Press.

Dill, J. S. (2007). Durkheim and Dewey and the challenge of contemporary moral education. *Journal of Moral Education, 36*(2), 221–237.

Doob, C. B. (2015). *Social inequality and social stratification in US society.* New York, NY: Routledge.

Duckworth, A. L. (2016). *Grit: The power of passion and perseverance.* New York, NY: Scribner.

Duckworth, A. L., & Gross, J. J. (2014). Self-control and grit: Related but separable determinants of success. *Current Directions in Psychological Science, 23*(5), 319–325.

Duckworth, A. L., Kirby, T. A., Tsukayama, E., Berstein, H., & Ericsson, K. A. (2011). Deliberate practice spells success: Why grittier competitors triumph at the National Spelling Bee. *Social Psychological and Personality Science, 2*(2), 174–181.

Duckworth, A. L., Peterson, C., Matthews, M. D., & Kelly, D. R. (2007). Grit: Perseverance and passion for long-term goals. *Journal of Personality and Social Psychology, 92*(6), 1087–1101.

Duckworth, A. L., White, R. E., Matteucci, A. J., Shearer, A., & Gross, J. J. (2016). A stitch in time: Strategic self-control in high school and college students. *Journal of Educational Psychology, 108*(3), 329–341.

Duffey, T., & Somody, C. (2011). The role of relational-cultural theory in mental health counseling. *Journal of Mental Health Counseling, 33*(3), 223–242.

Duncan-Andrade, J. M. R., & Morrell, E. (2008). *The art of critical pedagogy: Possibilities for moving from theory to practice in urban schools* (Vol. 285). New York, NY: Peter Lang.

Duncan, G. J., & Murnane, R. J. (2014). *Restoring opportunity: The crisis of inequality and the challenge for American education.* Cambridge, MA: Harvard Education Press.

Durkheim, E. (1938). *The rules of sociological method* (G. Catlin, Trans.). Glencoe, IL: Free Press.

Durkheim, E. (2008). *The elementary forms of the religious life.* New York, NY: Oxford University Press. (Original work published 1912)

Dweck, C. S. (2008). Can personality be changed? The role of beliefs in personality and change. *Current Directions in Psychological Science, 17*(6), 391–394.

Dworsky, A., & Courtney, M. E. (2010). The risk of teenage pregnancy among transitioning foster youth: Implications for extending state care beyond age 18. *Children and Youth Services Review, 32*(10), 1351–1356.

Dyrbye, L. N., West, C. P., Satele, D., Boone, S., Tan, L., Sloan, J., & Shanafelt, T. D. (2014). Burnout among US medical students, residents, and early career physicians relative to the general US population. *Academic Medicine, 89*(3), 443–451.

EdBuild. (2019). *Nonwhite schools get $23 billion less than White districts despite serving the same number of students.* Retrieved from https://edbuild.org/content/23-billion

Embich, J. L. (2001). The relationship of secondary special education teachers' roles and factors that lead to professional burnout. *Teacher Education and Special Education, 24*(1), 58–69.

Emirbayer, M., & Mische, A. (1998). What is agency? *American Journal of Sociology, 103*(4), 962–1023.

Ewing, E. L. (2018). *Ghosts in the schoolyard: Racism and school closings on Chicago's South Side*. Chicago, IL: University of Chicago Press.

Farber, B. A. (1991). *Crisis in education: Stress and burnout in the American teacher*. San Francisco, CA: Jossey-Bass.

Feldman Farb, A., & Margolis, A. L. (2016). The teen pregnancy prevention program (2010–2015): Synthesis of impact findings. *American Journal of Public Health, 106*(Suppl 1), S9–S15.

Fernandes-Alcantara, A. (2018). *Federal approaches to teen pregnancy prevention*. Washington, DC: Congressional Research Service.

Fine, M. (1991). *Framing dropouts: Notes on the politics of an urban high school*. Albany, NY: SUNY Press.

Fisher, J. F. (2018). *Who you know: Unlocking innovations that expand students' networks*. Hoboken, NJ: John Wiley & Sons.

Ford, D. Y., & Grantham, T. C. (2003). Providing access for culturally diverse gifted students: From deficit to dynamic thinking. *Theory into Practice, 42*(3), 217–225.

Freire, P. (1972). *Pedagogy of the oppressed* (Reprint ed.; M. Bergman Ramos, Trans.). New York, NY: Herder and Herder. (Original work published 1968)

Frey, W. H. (2018). *Diversity explosion: How new racial demographics are remaking America*. Washington, DC: Brookings Institution Press.

Fruchter, N., Hester, M., Mokhtar, C., & Shahn, Z. (2012). *Is demography still destiny? Neighborhood demographics and public high school students' readiness for college in New York City*. (Research and policy brief). Providence, RI: Brown Institute, Annenberg Institute for School Reform.

Fuller, J. B., & Raman, M. (2017). *Dismissed by degrees: How degree inflation is undermining US competitiveness and hurting America's middle class*. Cambridge, MA: Accenture, Grads of Life, Harvard Business School.

Furman Center for Real Estate & Urban Policy. (2017). New York City neighborhood data profiles. Retreived from furmancenter.org/neighborhoods

Gabrielson, R., Sagara, E., & Jones, R. G. (2014, October 10). Deadly force, in black and white. Retrieved from www.propublica.org/article/deadly-force-in-black-and-white

Garner, R., & Scott, G. M. (2013). *Doing qualitative research: Designs, methods, and techniques*. Upper Saddle River, NJ: Pearson Education.

Gaydosh, L., Schorpp, K. M., Chen, E., Miller, G. E., & Harris, K. M. (2018). College completion predicts lower depression but higher metabolic syndrome among disadvantaged minorities in young adulthood. *Proceedings of the National Academy of Sciences, 115*(1), 109–114.

Geertz, C. (1973). *The interpretation of cultures* (Vol. 5019). New York, NY: Basic Books.

George, D. (2016, November 13). How mindfulness practices are changing an inner-city school. *The Washington Post*. Retrieved from www.washingtonpost.com/local/education/how-mindfulness-practices-are-changing-an-inner-city-school/2016/11/13/7b4a274a-a833-11e6-ba59-a7d93165c6d4_story.html?utm_term=.c4bc0b44e216.

Genovese, E. D. (1976). *Roll, Jordan, roll: The world the slaves made*. New York, NY: Vintage.

Gilligan, C. (2015). The Listening Guide method of psychological inquiry. *Qualitative Psychology, 2*(1), 69–77.

Giroux, H. A. (1983). *Theory and resistance in education: A pedagogy for the opposition*. South Hadley, MA: Bergin & Garvey.

Gladwell, M. (2008). *Outliers: The story of success*. London, England: Hachette UK.

Gold, H. (2014, November 12). Why does a campus police department have jurisdiction over 65,000 Chicago residents? Retrieved from www.vice.com/en_us/article/4w7p8b/why-does-a-campus-police-department-have-jurisdiction-over-65000-chicago-residents-1112

Gonzales, R. G. (2016). *Lives in limbo: Undocumented and coming of age in America*. Berkeley, CA: University of California Press.

Gorski, P. C. (2011). Unlearning deficit ideology and the scornful gaze: Thoughts on authenticating the class discourse in education. *Counterpoints, 402,* 152–173.

Gorski, P. C. (2016). Poverty and the ideological imperative: A call to unhook from deficit and grit ideology and to strive for structural ideology in teacher education. *Journal of Education for Teaching, 42*(4), 378–386.

Griffee, D. T. (2005). Research tips: Interview data collection. *Journal of Developmental Education, 28*(3), 36–37.

Grimm, P. (2010). Social desirability bias. In *Wiley international encyclopedia of marketing.* Retrieved from www.researchgate.net/publication/277708190_Social_Desirability_Bias

Hanselman, P., Bruch, S. K., Gamoran, A., & Borman, G. D. (2014). Threat in context: School moderation of the impact of social identity threat on racial/ethnic achievement gaps. *Sociology of Education, 87*(2), 106–124

Harris, A. L. (2011). *Kids don't want to fail.* Cambridge, MA: Harvard University Press.

Hartley, M. T. (2011). Examining the relationships between resilience, mental health, and academic persistence in undergraduate college students. *Journal of American College Health, 59*(7), 596–604.

Heckman, J. J. (1995). Lessons from the Bell Curve. *Journal of Political Economy, 103*(5), 1091–1120.

Henry, W. A., III. (1995). *In defense of elitism.* New York, NY: Anchor.

Henshaw, S. K. (1998). Unintended pregnancy in the United States. *Family Planning Perspectives, 30*(1), 24–46.

Herrnstein, R. J., & Murray, C. (2010). *The bell curve: Intelligence and class structure in American life.* New York, NY: Simon & Schuster.

Hetherington, E. M. (2014). *Coping with divorce, single parenting, and remarriage: A risk and resiliency perspective.* London, England: Psychology Press.

Hitlin, S., & Kirkpatrick Johnson, M. (2015). Reconceptualizing agency within the life course: The power of looking ahead. *American Journal of Sociology, 120*(5), 1429–1472.

Hitlin, S., & Kwon, H. W. (2016). Agency across the life course. In M. J. Shanahan, J. T. Mortimer, & M. K. Johnson (Eds.), *Handbook of the life course* (pp. 431–449). New York, NY: Springer.

Holland, S. P., & Cohen, C. J. (2005). *Black queer studies: A critical anthology.* Durham, NC: Duke University Press.

hooks, b. (1992). *Representing whiteness in the black imagination.* New York, NY: Routledge.

Horning, K., Lindgren, M., & Schliesman, M. (2014). *A few observations on publishing in 2012.* Madison, WI: Cooperative Children's Book Center.

Huang, C. Y., Costeines, J., Kaufman, J. S., & Ayala, C. (2014). Parenting stress, social support, and depression for ethnic minority adolescent mothers: Impact on child development. *Journal of Child and Family Studies, 23*(2), 255–262.

Hughes, L. (1959). *Selected poems of Langston Hughes.* New York, NY: Alfred A. Knopf.

Hoover, H. (1934).*The challenge to liberty.* New York, NY: Charles Scribner's Sons.

Hulbert, A. (2011). *Raising America: Experts, parents, and a century of advice about children.* New York, NY: Vintage.

Hurrelmann, K. (1988). *Social structure and personality development: The individual as a productive processor of reality.* Cambridge, England: Cambridge University Press.

Jackson, P. W. (1990). *Life in classrooms.* New York, NY: Teachers College Press.

Jacobs, S. R., & Dodd, D. (2003). Student burnout as a function of personality, social support, and workload. *Journal of College Student Development, 44*(3), 291–303.

James S. A. (1994). John Henryism and the health of African-Americans. *Culture, Medicine and Psychiatry,18,* 163–182. doi:10.1007/BF01379448

Johnson Jr, O. (2014). Still separate, still unequal: The relation of segregation in neighborhoods and schools to education inequality. *The Journal of Negro Education, 83*(3), 199–215.

Kao, G. (2004). Parental influences on the educational outcomes of immigrant youth. *International Migration Review, 38*(2), 427–449.

Karcher, M. J. (2008). The cross-age mentoring program: A developmental intervention for promoting students' connectedness across grade levels. *Professional School Counseling, 12*(2), 137–143.

Kaye, K., Suellentrop, K., & Sloup, C. (2009). *The fog zone: How misperceptions, magical thinking, and ambivalence put young adults at risk for unplanned pregnancy.* Washington, DC: The National Campaign to Prevent Teen and Unplanned Pregnancy.

Kelley, R. D. (1996). *Race rebels: Culture, politics, and the Black working class.* New York, NY. Simon and Schuster.

Kenney, A. M. (1987). Teen pregnancy: An issue for schools. *Phi Delta Kappan, 68*(10), 728–736.

Khan, S. R. (2012). *Privilege: The making of an adolescent elite at St. Paul's School.* Princeton, NJ: Princeton University Press.

Kim, K. A., Sax, L. J., Lee, J. J., & Hagedorn, L. S. (2010). Redefining nontraditional students: Exploring the self-perceptions of community college students. *Community College Journal of Research and Practice, 34*(5), 402–422.

King, M. L., Jr. (1965, June). *Remaining awake through a great revolution* (Commencement Address, Oberlin College). Oberlin College Archives. Retrieved from www2.oberlin.edu/external/EOG/BlackHistoryMonth/MLK/CommAddress.html

King, M. L., Jr. (2012). Letter from Birmingham jail. In R. Gottlieb (Ed.), *Liberating faith: Religious voices for justice, peace, & ecological wisdom* (pp. 177–187). Lanham, MD: Rowman and Littlefield Publishers.

Kozol, J. (2012). *Savage inequalities: Children in America's schools.* New York, NY: Broadway Books.

Kropf, N. P., & Kolomer, S. (2004). Grandparents raising grandchildren: A diverse population. *Journal of Human Behavior in the Social Environment, 9*(4), 65–83.

Kundu, A. (2015, October 28). Policing schools and dividing the nation [Blog post]. Huffington Post. Retrieved from www.huffpost.com/entry/policing-schools-and-divi_b_8400426

Kundu, A. (2016). Roses in concrete: A perspective on how agency and grit can foster the success of all students, especially those most disadvantaged. *The Journal of School & Society, 3*(2), 18–21.

Kundu, A. (2017). Grit and agency: A framework for helping students in poverty to achieve academic greatness. *National Youth-At-Risk Journal, 2*(2), 69.

Kundu, A. (2018). *Adding a social perspective to grit: How students with disadvantages navigate obstacles and gain agency* (Doctoral dissertation, New York University). Available from ProQuest Dissertations and Theses database.

Kundu, A. (2019). Understanding college "burnout" from a social perspective: Reigniting the agency of low-income racial minority strivers towards achievement. *Urban Review, 51*(5), 677–698.

Kundu, A., & Noguera, P. (2014). Why America's infatuation with "grit" can't solve our educational dilemmas. *Virginia Policy Review, 11,* 49–53.

Kwon, H. W. (2017). The sociology of grit: Exploring grit as a sociological variable and its potential role in social stratification. *Sociology Compass, 11*(12), 1–13.

Ladson-Billings, G. (1997). It doesn't add up: African American students' mathematical achievement. *Journal for Research in Mathematics Education, 28*(6), 697–708.

Ladson-Billings, G. (2006). From the achievement gap to the education debt: Understanding achievement in US schools. *Educational Researcher, 35*(7), 3–12.

Ladson-Billings, G. (2009). *The dreamkeepers: Successful teachers of African-American children.* San Francisco, CA: John Wiley & Sons.

Langley, C., Barbee, A. P., Antle, B., Christensen, D., Archuleta, A., Sar, B. K., . . . Borders, K. (2015). Enhancement of reducing the risk for the 21st century: Improvement to a curriculum developed to prevent teen pregnancy and STI transmission. *American Journal of Sexuality Education, 10*(1), 40–69.

Lareau, A. (1987). Social class differences in family-school relationships: The importance of cultural capital. *Sociology of Education, 60*(2), 73–85.

Lareau, A. (2002). Invisible inequality: Social class and childrearing in Black families and White families. *American Sociological Review, 67*(5), 747–776.

Lareau, A. (2011). *Unequal childhoods: Class, race, and family life.* Berkeley: University of California Press.

Lareau, A., & Weininger, E. B. (2003). Cultural capital in educational research: A critical assessment. *Theory and Society, 32*(5–6), 567–606.

Lee, J. S., & Bowen, N. K. (2006). Parent involvement, cultural capital, and the achievement gap among elementary school children. *American Educational Research Journal, 43*(2), 193–218.

Lewis, A. E. (2003). *Race in the schoolyard: Negotiating the color line in classrooms and communities.* New Brunswick, NJ: Rutgers University Press.

Lifflander, A., Gaydos, L. M. D., & Rowland Hogue, C. J. (2007). Circumstances of pregnancy: Low income women in Georgia describe the difference between planned and unplanned pregnancies. *Maternal and Child Health Journal, 11*(1), 81–89.

Lipman, P. (1998). *Race, class, and power in school restructuring.* Albany, NY: SUNY Press.

Love, N. (2009). Parents Involved in Community Schools v. Seattle School District No. 1: The application of strict scrutiny to race-conscious student assignment policies in K-12 public schools. *Boston College Third World Law Journal, 29*(1), 115–149.

Lucas, G. M., Gratch, J., Cheng, L., & Marsella, S. (2015). When the going gets tough: Grit predicts costly perseverance. *Journal of Research in Personality, 59*, 15–22.

MacLeod, J. (1987). *Ain't no makin' it: Leveled aspirations in a low-income community.* Boulder, CO: Westview Press.

Mahnken, K. (2018, April 18). At ASU-GSV, Angela Duckworth talks grit and the challenges of building a movement: 'Education is so hard that it tests even my own grit.' Retrieved from www.the74million.org/article/at-asu-gsv-angela-duckworth-talks-grit-and-the -challenges-of-building-a-movement-education-is-so-hard-that-it-tests-even-my-own-grit/

Marsh, J. (2011). *Class dismissed: Why we cannot teach or learn our way out of inequality.* New York, NY: NYU Press.

Maslach, C., Jackson, S. E., Leiter, M. P., Schaufeli, W. B., & Schwab, R. L. (1986). *Maslach burnout inventory* (Vol. 21, pp. 3463–3464). Palo Alto, CA: Consulting Psychologists Press.

McCabe, J. M. (2016). *Connecting in college: How friendship networks matter for academic and social success.* Chicago, IL: University of Chicago Press.

McGee, E. O., & Stovall, D. (2015). Reimagining critical race theory in education: Mental health, healing, and the pathway to liberatory praxis. *Educational Theory, 65*(5), 491–511.

McLanahan, S., & Sandefur, G. (1994). *Growing up with a single parent: What hurts, what helps.* Cambridge, MA: Harvard University Press.

McWhorter, J. H. (2000). *Losing the race: Self-sabotage in Black America.* New York, NY: The Free Press.

Mead, G. H. (1934). *Mind, self and society.* Chicago, IL: University of Chicago Press.

Musca, T. (Producer), & Menéndez, R. (Director). (1988). *Stand and deliver* [Film]. Warner Bros.

Mercer, J. (2007). The challenges of insider research in educational institutions: Wielding a double-edged sword and resolving delicate dilemmas. *Oxford Review of Education, 33*(1), 1–17.

Mickelson, R. A. (1990). The attitude-achievement paradox among Black adolescents. *Sociology of Education, 63*(1), 44–61.

Miles, M., Huberman, M., & Saldana, J. (2013). *Qualitative data analysis: A methods sourcebook.* Thousand Oaks, CA: Sage.

Milner, H. R., IV. (2012). But what is urban education? *Urban Education, 47*(3), 556–561. doi:10.1177/0042085912447516

Mohammed, D. (2016, Nov. 30). Stop fetishizing minority students as superhuman poverty survivors. *The Tab.* Retrieved from thetab.com/us/columbia/2016/11/22/minority-students-columbia-university-3694

Morrell, E. (2004). *Becoming critical researchers: Literacy and empowerment for urban youth* (Vol. 227). New York, NY: Peter Lang.

Nagaoka, J., Farrington, C. A., Ehrlich, S. B., & Heath, R. D. (2015). *Foundations for young adult success: A developmental framework* (Concept Paper for Research and Practice). Chicago, IL: University of Chicago Consortium on Chicago School Research.

Neal, J. W., & Neal, Z. P. (2013). Nested or networked? Future directions for ecological systems theory. *Social Development, 22*(4), 722–737. doi:10.1111/sode.12018

Neale, B., & Clayton, C. L. (2014). Young parenthood and cross-generational relationships: The perspectives of young fathers. In J. Holland & R. Edwards (Eds.), *Understanding families over time* (pp. 69–87). London, England: Palgrave Macmillan.

New York City Department of Education. (2018). *DOE data at a glance.* Retrieved from https://www.schools.nyc.gov/about-us/reports/doe-data-at-a-glance

New York City Department of Education. (2019). *NYC Men Teach.* Retrieved from www1.nyc.gov/site/ymi/teach/nyc-men-teach.page

Nieto, S., & Bode, P. (2005). *Affirming diversity: The sociopolitical context of multicultural education* (6th ed.). Boston, MA: Pearson Education.

Noguera, P. (2003). *City schools and the American dream: Reclaiming the promise of public education.* New York, NY: Teachers College Press.

Noguera, P. A. (2009). *The trouble with black boys: . . . And other reflections on race, equity, and the future of public education.* Hoboken, NJ: John Wiley & Sons.

Nonko, E. (2019, April 3). *The study group bringing bell hooks to prisons.* Retrieved from nextcity.org/daily/entry/the-study-group-bringing-bell-hooks-to-prisons

Obama, B. (2017). *Farewell address.* Retrieved from www.nytimes.com/2017/01/10/us/politics/obama-farewell-address-speech.html

Ogbu, J. U. (1992). Understanding cultural diversity and learning. *Educational Researcher, 21*(8), 5–14.

Ong, A. D., Bergeman, C. S., & Bisconti, T. L. (2004). The role of daily positive emotions during conjugal bereavement. *The Journals of Gerontology Series B: Psychological Sciences and Social Sciences, 59*(4), 168–176.

Patterson, O., & Fosse, E. (Eds.). (2015). *The cultural matrix.* Cambridge, MA: Harvard University Press.

Pell Institute. (2018). *Indicators of higher education equity in the United States: 2018 historical trend report.* Retrieved from http://pellinstitute.org/downloads/publications-Indicators_of_Higher_Education_Equity_in_the_US_2018_Historical_Trend_Report.pdf

Pomerantz, E. M., Ng, F. F. Y., Cheung, C. S.-S., & Qu, Y. (2014). Raising happy children who succeed in school: Lessons from China and the United States. *Child Development Perspectives, 8*(2), 71–76.

Pyrooz, D. C., McGloin, J. M., & Decker, S. H. (2017). Parenthood as a turning point in the life course for male and female gang members: A study of within-individual changes in gang membership and criminal behavior. *Criminology, 55*(4), 869–899.

Quaye, S. J., & Harper, S. R. (Eds.). (2014). *Student engagement in higher education: Theoretical perspectives and practical approaches for diverse populations.* London, England: Routledge.

Ransaw, T. S., & Majors, R. (Eds.). (2016). *Closing the education achievement gaps for African American males.* East Lansing, MI: Michigan State University Press.

Reardon, S. F., & Bischoff, K. (2011). Income inequality and income segregation. *American Journal of Sociology, 116*(4), 1092–1153.

Rios, V. M. (2012). Stealing a bag of potato chips and other crimes of resistance. *Contexts, 11*(1), 48–53.

Robbers, M. L. (2009). Facilitating fatherhood: A longitudinal examination of father involvement among young minority fathers. *Child and Adolescent Social Work Journal, 26*(2), 121–134.

Robinson, D. (2016, November 22). "Letter to My Younger Self." *The Players Tribune Online.* Retrieved from: www.theplayerstribune.com/en-us/articles/letter-to-my-younger-self-david-robinson

Roksa, J., Grodsky, E., Arum, R., & Gamoran, A. (2007). Changes in higher education and social stratification in the United States. In Y. Shavit, R. Arum, & R. Gamoran (Eds.), *Stratification in higher education* (pp. 165–191). Palo Alto, CA: Stanford University Press.

Rosenbaum, J. E., & Person, A. E. (2003). Beyond college for all: Policies and practices to improve transitions into college and jobs. *Professional School Counseling, 6*(4), 252–260.

Rosenbloom, S. R., & Way, N. (2004). Experiences of discrimination among African American, Asian American, and Latino adolescents in an urban high school. *Youth & Society, 35*(4), 420–451.

RTI International. (2019). *First-generation college students: Demographic characteristics and postsecondary enrollment.* Washington, DC: NASPA. Retrieved from firstgen.naspa.org/files/dmfile/FactSheet-01.pdf

Rubin, H. J., & Rubin, I. S. (2011). *Qualitative interviewing: The art of hearing data.* Thousand Oaks, CA: Sage.

Rumberger, R. W. (2011). *Dropping out.* Cambridge, MA: Harvard University Press.

Santiago, C. D., Wadsworth, M. E., & Stump, J. (2011). Socioeconomic status, neighborhood disadvantage, and poverty-related stress: Prospective effects on psychological syndromes among diverse low-income families. *Journal of Economic Psychology, 32*(2), 218–230.

Schacter, J., & Jo, B. (2005). Learning when school is not in session: A reading summer day-camp intervention to improve the achievement of exiting first-grade students who are economically disadvantaged. *Journal of Research in Reading, 28*(2), 158–169.

Seligman, M. E. (2002). Positive psychology, positive prevention, and positive therapy. In C. R. Snyder & S. J. Lopez (Eds.), *Handbook of positive psychology* (pp. 3–9). New York, NY: Oxford University Press.

Seligman, M. E. (2006). *Learned optimism: How to change your mind and your life.* New York, NY: Vintage.

Seligman, M. E., & Csikszentmihalyi, M. (2014). Positive psychology: An introduction. In M. Csikszentmihalyi (Ed.), *Flow and the foundations of positive psychology* (pp. 279–298). New York, NY: Springer.

Shanahan, M. J., Hofer, S. M., & Miech, R. A. (2003). Planful competence, the life course, and aging: Retrospect and prospect. In S. H. Zarit, L. I. Pearlin, & K. W. Schaie (Eds.), *Personal control in social and life course contexts* (pp. 189–211). New York, NY: Springer.

Sharkey, P. (2013). *Stuck in place: Urban neighborhoods and the end of progress toward racial equality.* Chicago, IL: University of Chicago Press.

Shechtman, N., DeBarger, A. H., Dornsife, C., Rosier, S., & Yarnall, L. (2013). *Promoting grit, tenacity, and perseverance: Critical factors for success in the 21st century.* Washington, DC: US Department of Education, Department of Educational Technology.

Shuger, L. (2012). *Teen pregnancy and high school dropout: What communities can do to address these issues.* Washington, DC: The National Campaign to Prevent Teen and Unplanned Pregnancy and America's Promise Alliance.

Sipsma, H., Biello, K. B., Cole-Lewis, H., & Kershaw, T. (2010). Like father, like son: The intergenerational cycle of adolescent fatherhood. *American Journal of Public Health, 100*(3), 517–524.

Slaughter-Defoe, D. T., & Rubin, H. H. (2001). A longitudinal case study of Head Start eligible children: Implications for urban education. *Educational Psychologist, 36*(1), 31–44.

Solomon-Fears, C. (2016). *The child support enforcement program: A legislative history.* Washington, DC: Congressional Research Service.

Steele, C. M., & Aronson, J. (2005). Stereotypes and the fragility of academic competence, motivation, and self-concept. In A. J. Elliot, C. S. Dweck, & D. S. Yeager (Eds.), *Handbook of competence and motivation* (pp. 436–455). New York, NY: The Guilford Press.

Swidler, A. (1986). Culture in action: Symbols and strategies. *American Sociological Review, 51*(2), 273–286.

Symonds, W. C., Schwartz, R., & Ferguson, R. F. (2011). *Pathways to prosperity: Meeting the challenge of preparing young Americans for the 21st century.* Cambridge, MA: Pathways to Prosperity Project, Harvard University Graduate School of Education.

Tinto, V. (1987). *Leaving college: Rethinking the causes and cures of student attrition.* Chicago, IL: University of Chicago Press.

Tough, P. (2013). *How children succeed: Grit, curiosity, and the hidden power of character.* New York, NY: Houghton Mifflin Harcourt.

Tough, P. (2016). *Helping children succeed: What works and why.* New York, NY: Houghton Mifflin Harcourt.

Trainor, A. A. (2010). Diverse approaches to parent advocacy during special education home–school interactions: Identification and use of cultural and social capital. *Remedial and Special Education, 31*(1), 34–47.

Treschan, L., & Lew, I. (2018). *Barriers to entry: Fewer out-of-school, out-of-work young adults, as warning signs emerge.* New York, NY: Community Service Society. Retrieved from jobsfirstnyc.org/wp-content/uploads/2019/05/Barriers-to-Entry-2018.pdf

Underwood, M., Satterthwait, L. D., & Bartlett, H. P. (2010). Reflexivity and minimization of the impact of age-cohort differences between researcher and research participants. *Qualitative Health Research, 20*(11), 1585–1595.

U.S. Census Bureau. (n.d.). *Thematic maps.* Retrieved from https://www.census.gov/geo/maps-data/maps/thematic.html

Vainio, M. M., & Daukantaitė, D. (2016). Grit and different aspects of well-being: Direct and indirect relationships via sense of coherence and authenticity. *Journal of Happiness Studies, 17*(5), 2119–2147.

Valencia, R. R. (2002). "Mexican Americans don't value education!"—On the basis of the myth, mythmaking, and debunking. *Journal of Latinos and Education, 1*(2), 81–103.

Veiga, C. (2017). Prayers, precision and push-ups: Special ed teacher puts his background to work in the classroom. *The Education Digest, 83*(2), 21.

Waldrop, D. P., & Weber, J. A. (2001). From grandparent to caregiver: The stress and satisfaction of raising grandchildren. *Families in Society, 82*(5), 461–472.

West, M. R., Kraft, M. A., Finn, A. S., Martin, R. E., Duckworth, A. L., Gabrieli, C. F., & Gabrieli, J. D. (2016). Promise and paradox: Measuring students' non-cognitive skills and the impact of schooling. *Educational Evaluation and Policy Analysis, 38*(1), 148–170.

Willis, P. (1977). *Learning to labour: How working class kids get working class jobs.* London, England: Saxon House.

Wyman, S. L. (1993). *How to respond to your culturally diverse student population.* Alexandria, VA: Association for Supervision and Curriculum Development.

Yoshikawa, H. (2011). *Immigrants raising citizens: Undocumented parents and their children.* New York, NY: Russell Sage Foundation.

Yosso, T. J. (2005). Whose culture has capital? A critical race theory discussion of community cultural wealth. *Race, Ethnicity and Education, 8*(1), 69–91.

Zernike, K. (2016, February, 29). Testing for joy and grit? Schools nationwide push to measure students' emotional skills. *The New York Times.* Retrieved from www.nytimes.com/2016/03/01/us/testing-for-joy-and-grit-schools-nationwide-push-to-measure-students-emotional-skills.html

Index

About the Author

Anindya Kundu, PhD, is a sociologist who studies the contexts that allow youth and young adults to thrive. He is currently a senior fellow at the Center for Urban Research at the Graduate Center, within the City University of New York (CUNY). Anindya also serves as a member of the New York City Department of Education Career and Technical Education Advisory Council. He received his bachelor's from the University of Chicago and his PhD in sociology of education from New York University (NYU), where he was an award-winning educator. Anindya taught undergraduate and graduate level courses at NYU, including American Dilemmas: Race, Inequality, and the Promise of Public Education; Research in Minority and Urban Education; and Education as a Social Institution. He enjoys connecting research to practice; his work has been featured in NPR Education, MSNBC, and Huffington Post. Anindya has given two official TED Talks, each with over 1.5 million views.